The Data Governance Imperative

A business strategy for corporate data

The Data Governance Imperative

A business strategy for corporate data

STEVE SARSFIELD

IT Governance Publishing

IT Governance Publishing
IT Governance Limited
Unit 3, Clive Court
Bartholomew's Walk
Cambridgeshire Business Park
Ely
Cambridgeshire
CB7 4EH
United Kingdom

www.itgovernance.co.uk

© Steve Sarsfield 2009
The author has asserted the rights of the author under the Copyright, Designs and Patents Act, 1988, to be identified as the author of this work.

First published in the United Kingdom in 2009
by IT Governance Publishing.

ISBN: 978-1-84928-012-9

FOREWORD

Congratulations! By buying this book, you have realized the importance of corporate information. Every byte of data that resides inside your company, and some that resides outside its walls, has the potential to make you stronger by giving you the agility, speed and intelligence that none of your competitors yet have.

With your pursuit of a data governance initiative, you have reached a level of corporate maturity that many others have not achieved. That maturity will set you apart from the competition today and will keep you competitive when data governance becomes a matter-of-fact component of corporate stewardship.

With your new attention to corporate information, you will be better able to comply with worldwide laws that govern corporations. The ability to generate accurate business intelligence, accurate financial reports, and understand your business relies on better processes and personal commitment to clean data. Corporate officers will applaud the availability of solid business metrics and not having to rely so much on instinct. With attention to data governance, your customers will be delighted as you better understand their needs, handle support issues more smoothly and are better able deliver "green" programs as a responsible corporation of our fragile world.

But in order to tap into this strength, you need to take a proactive approach to managing the data. Data does not govern itself and valuable assets like corporate information need to be managed.

Foreword

Today, there are many technical articles, books and blog entries about data governance and related topics. This book is different. It's a business person's view of data governance. This book covers both strategies and tactics around managing a data governance initiative.

If you've ever fancied yourself as your company's data champion, you'll know that it is often difficult to get traction and build a critical mass of support on data governance. Let's face it, there's plenty of day-to-day work to get done and there's always an excuse to put off data governance for tomorrow. Despite the strategic and competitive advantages of a planned data management program, it may take effort, a strong effort, to get others to see that it is absolutely the right thing to do for the corporation and the world. In this book, we'll talk about being a change agent in your corporation and breaking through those barriers.

Once your data management program begins to build support, the next hurdle to overcome is to understand exactly how to begin. Most companies that have been successful in data governance programs start with small, high-impact projects, track results, and market those results to the company. We'll talk about the processes you can put in place to accomplish all of that. We'll also talk about the tools you can use to make the project more efficient.

Finally, and most importantly, people are really the change agents in a data governance initiative. It'll be important to know what a data governance team looks like and what their responsibilities should be. This book will cover strategies and tactics for managing a team. Again, tools can play an important role here, too.

Foreword

So, welcome to the world of data governance, and congratulations on being business users, executives and data champions that have the courage and tenacity to be an agent of change for your corporation.

PREFACE

In so much of the information that is available on data governance, the experts all say that it is not a challenge solely for the IT team – it's a business issue. They say that business users and technical users must come together, work hand in hand, to solve the issues of data quality. Data governance is about improving processes with help from people.

But if data governance is a business issue, why are there so many technical books on the subject? Why do so many of the experts in the field go on to talk about topics like metadata management, master data management, database schemas and other technical components of data governance?

Data governance is about changing the hearts and minds of your company to see the value of information quality. It's a process that matures an organization, making it more efficient and more valuable. It's about educating people to do the right thing for the sake of the organization. A relatively small component of data governance is about the technology.

Many companies never start the process because they start with the technology and they fail to see the business value that can be achieved by process improvement. It is because of this that budget requests for data governance project funding is rejected. Those who desire to evolve their company are often hindered by lack of data governance expertise and an immature corporate view of data management. The technical solutions to information quality issues are never considered because of the lack of understanding of business issues surrounding data governance.

Today, we know that before you install even a single piece of software, the business has much work to do to ensure success in data governance and information quality. Project teams must prepare, plan, set goals and staffing levels appropriately, and track and promote progress.

When it comes to justifying the costs of data governance to their organization, building organizational processes, learning how to staff initiatives, understanding the role and importance of technologies, and dealing with corporate politics, there is little information available. This book will help readers pioneer data governance initiatives, breaking through political barriers by shining a light on the benefits of corporate information quality. This book is designed to give data governance team members insight into the art of starting data governance.

In my years working at a major data quality vendor, I have been exposed to many projects in Fortune 1000 companies worldwide. I've seen what makes for good data governance and what process is likely to fail. I've seen that successful strategies for data governance are not all the same, yet there are common threads to success within and across the industry.

As part of my work, I am also a student of data governance and data quality strategies. I have followed the evolution of project-focused data quality initiatives of the 1990s into the enterprise-wide initiatives and information quality centers of excellence of today. I write and read white papers on information quality. I have delivered and viewed hundreds of web seminars and live presentations on data governance.

All of these experiences have been cold filtered and amalgamated into this book.

I decided to write this book because I saw a common recurring question that arose during discussions about data governance. How do I get my boss to believe that data governance is important? How do I work with my colleagues to build better information and a better company? How do I break through the barriers to data governance like getting money, resources and expertise to accomplish the task? The strategies for doing all of those things were scattered and rare.

This book does not focus on the technical aspects of data governance, although technologies are discussed. There are some great books on the technology of data governance in the market today. They usually have terms like "MDM" and "CDI" in the title, since these can be enabling technologies for data governance. Instead, this book should be used by business and IT teams such as:

- Data governance teams – those looking for direction/validation in starting a corporate data governance initiative.
- Business stakeholders – those working in marketing, sales, finance and other business roles who need to understand the goals and functions of a data governance team.
- C-level executives – those looking to learn about the benefits of data governance without having to read excessive technical jargon, or even those who need to be convinced that data governance is the right thing to do.
- IT executives – those who believe in the power of information quality but have faced challenges in convincing others in their corporation of its value.

If you promote an IT view of data governance, the message will tend to fall flat. The tips you'll get from my book will help you speak the business-speak of those who sign your purchase orders.

The process of writing this book took longer than I expected, but I did learn something very valuable about myself, and it's not something that's easy to admit: I have a passion for data governance and data management practices.

How many children or college graduates have aspirations of becoming a data management professional? When my friends and I were growing up, we had aspirations to be millionaires, doctors, firemen or lawyers. As a child, I toyed with the idea of becoming an American Football NFL wide receiver like the great Lynn Swann. However, two left feet and two left hands eventually led me into the data management world.

It's a romance that is rarely love at first sight … rather it grows on you. When you get involved with managing corporate data, you'll begin to realize the power it has. You'll love data governance for the efficiencies it brings, and for the impact it will have on your organization as it becomes more competitive. You'll love data governance for the assurance that you'll be ready for any future business change, merger or regulatory action. This wonderful and unabashed confidence becomes part of the lifeblood of your organization, feeding your whole organization with solid, actionable information. So, are you ready?

ABOUT THE AUTHOR

Steve Sarsfield is a leading expert in data quality and data governance, focusing on the business perspectives that are important to data champions, front-office employees, and executives. Steve runs an award-winning and world-recognized blog called the Data Governance and Data Quality Insider and is a popular public speaker on the topic, having delivered countless presentations at industry conferences and college campuses throughout the United States. He is a member of the organizing committee for the 2009 MIT Information Quality Industry Symposium (IQIS) which facilitates vibrant discussion among practitioners and academicians on how to improve the quality of information. Steve draws practical wisdom and inspiration from his colleagues at Harte-Hanks Trillium Software and its customers as they venture into their own data governance projects.

The Data Governance and Data Quality Insider Blog can be found at *http://data-governance.blogspot.com*.

ACKNOWLEDGEMENTS

If there's one thing I have tried to accomplish with this book, it is to bridge the gap between technology and business, and I have a lot of people on both sides of the equation to thank.

I'd like to thank my colleagues at Harte-Hanks Trillium Software, who have stirred my imagination and given me the confidence to put pen to paper. I'd also like to thank the many great customers of Trillium Software who have shared some of their data governance initiatives. You've taught me a lot about real-world data management.

The world of data management is a special community, so I would like to thank them for knowledge shared over the years that I'm sure in some ways has been woven into the concepts within this book. If you've ever written a blog entry, given a presentation at a trade show, given a webinar, written a white paper or a book on data governance, thanks for sharing your ideas with us.

Thanks to the people of Costa Rica for their excellent coffee and the people of Austria for creating Red Bull. The world is more beautiful when it is caffeinated.

Most of all, I'd like to thank my wife, Valerie, who was my inspiration and my determination to finish this book. Writing a long manuscript like this is more time consuming than I thought. Thanks for supporting me and being so positive.

CONTENTS

Contents

Contents

CHAPTER 1: THE NEED FOR DATA GOVERNANCE

Today, most executives and business workers realize that their success is increasingly tied to the quality of their information. Companies rely on data to make significant decisions that can affect customer service, regulatory compliance, the supply chain and many other areas. As your company collects more and more data about customers, products, suppliers, transactions and billing, it becomes more difficult to accurately maintain that information without a centralized approach and a team devoted to the data management mission.

Companies usually find themselves in need of data governance as a remedy for growing pains. In fact, analysts like Gartner Research and Forrester agree that there is a data governance maturation process (maturity model) that describes a company's evolutionary process with regard to data governance. A company can evolve though stages. The first stages starts with the wild, wild west of data management where everyone makes their own rules and owns their own data. In stage one there is no cohesive plan for data, nor is there anyone particularly responsible for managing data.

Eventually, the company runs into difficulties and this forces it to evolve through a maturation process, eventually finishing in a governed data management atmosphere where business users and technologists form a cross-functional team that collaborates on data management. At its height, the most evolved companies will have support from executive management and the entire company to define reusable processes for data governance and a center of excellence is formed around it.

But before a company can get to a more evolved data management strategy, it's important to look at how most companies get into a data management crisis – what leads a company to need to consider data governance?

Sins of the past

To really understand why your company is in need of data governance, you have to go back to the beginning. You have to go back to the time when your company was just starting out. You have to remember when you, as a company, were full of hope and your new idea was just so innovative and needed in the marketplace. Your product was your main focus. Database systems and applications added certain efficiencies that fostered your growth.

Slowly, your company began to build customers. The customers may have been from your local area at first, but slowly the circle began to grow – first locally, then regionally, then nationwide, then worldwide. Life is good when your market share grows as the world opens up for business.

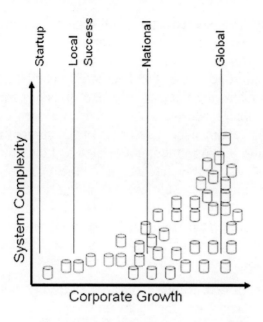

Figure 1: Growth/system complexity

The challenges in growing so quickly never seemed to be with the IT system, but were more about how to meet demand of product, how to expand markets, and how to acquire companies to speed growth. Rarely does a small- to medium-sized company give thought about the day that they will become a Fortune 500 company, at least not from a systems perspective. It doesn't often consider the data challenges of becoming a large company either; it's usually cheaper and easier to fix an immediate problem with glue and duct tape than it is to think about it strategically. Management and employees alike encouraged technologists to implement the quick fixes that kept the wheels running and shied away from replacing the wheels while the vehicle was speeding down the motorway.

What may have started as a small regional manufacturing company expanded into a worldwide manufacturing company with sales offices all over North and South America, Europe, Asia, the Pacific Rim and the Middle East. For managing data, each of the divisions formulated processes that made sense for them and met their own needs. The data management needs of the corporation were not available and/or not communicated and therefore took a backseat to the immediate needs of the business unit. If your company was clairvoyant enough to have a data management vision, and almost no small- or medium-sized company does, the rate of expansion and divisional structure that your company set up made it difficult to meet those needs.

Data silos formed. Rather than a structure that talks to re-use of data across the company, each business unit developed their own strategies for managing data. Each business unit hired their own data management resources – some who preferred to use Microsoft® SQL Server®, some who were Oracle® proficient, and some who liked to manage data on the mainframe in DB2®, to name just a few. The processes for maintaining clean data were just as diverse; after all, the definition of "clean data" varied from business unit to business unit. Data from the European sales division could look quite different from the data from the North American manufacturing business unit.

As data anomalies arose, some business units decided to address issues by writing their own code to fix data management problems. Whether the ad hoc solution was code within a database application, within a unique data management tool or as a custom application, the chasm of incongruent data continued to widen. The ad hoc code was designed to fix the business unit's problems, not address the needs of the enterprise.

As your company grew, there may have been acquisitions and mergers. These are good for growth, but bad for the complexity of enterprise systems and corporate processes. More and more incongruent data made its way into your systems with absolutely no foresight into the data needs of the enterprise.

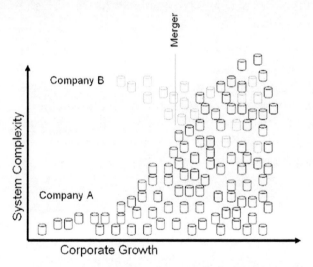

Figure 2: Mergers drive system complexity

This brings us to where most companies that are looking at data governance are today – silos of incongruent and disparate data with very little interaction between them.

Where are the metrics?

After this rapid growth and acquisition period, at some point someone important, usually an officer of the company, begins to ask some simple questions like:

- How many widgets did we sell last month worldwide?
- How many widgets are in inventory?
- Who is our best customer?
- Is all of our business profitable? What business/product is most profitable?

These are just the simple questions, all of them requiring clean, accurate data from across the entire company to answer accurately. However, with so much data in so many systems, it's extremely difficult to find the answers. On top of the sheer number of data sources, this rapid data growth and natural complexity has led to vision-blocking factors that interfere with gaining intelligence about your company. These factors might include:

- Lack of standards – People may have the best intentions, but the organization has not set up worldwide standards for data. Instead, the divisions enter data in a self-serving manner, entering only what's important to them.
- Typos and duplicates – As people enter data into your systems, they make mistakes. They transpose characters, type data into the wrong fields, and duplicate data, making it difficult to match up the same items from different systems.
- Platforms – Enterprise platforms may be diverse across your organization to include SAP®, Oracle/Siebel®, Tibco® or SalesForce®. When you grew, you acquired companies that used different enterprise applications and now those applications have to share data in order for

you to get the information you need. The business units also made decisions on platforms that were inconsistent, making decisions solely about their own needs.

- Language – As you grew, the global divisions used their own languages in the systems. This is troublesome especially for manufacturing. What exists in one system as "carrot" exists in another as the Dutch "biet" or even the Chinese "胡萝卜," making it very difficult to determine how many carrots you use worldwide.

- Competing information quality processes – Seeing the need for better data, individuals within divisions may choose to fix the data with their own data quality processes. However, the needs of the entire enterprise are rarely considered, and other divisions in the company may have their own ideas about what constitutes proper information quality.

- Code pages – Data may exist in different code pages. You may have heard of terms like ASCII, Unicode, and EBCDIC. Each of these code pages has a different way to represent the letter "a" for example. These are usually tied to the platforms like Windows®, Unix and mainframe platforms, or may be a factor of the region of the world in which the data originated. Reconciliation of the data in different code pages is necessary for database consolidation or even just getting metrics out of the systems.

- Data age and reliability – Data may be too old to be reliable, but it's hard to know without a deep look. Unfortunately, the employee that understood COBOL copybooks retired long ago.

- Unknown data – No one knows what the data is, or if it's relevant. The data may be an important customer list from an acquisition, but anyone who knows that left your company six months ago.

All of these factors block your company from knowing the very basics of your business. You can't go to one source to find the information you need to know.

Unnecessary complexity

To solve this problem, a common practice for companies is to hire analysts to sort it all out. These analysts generally come from the finest business schools in the world, spending many years in school learning about business and earning an MBA degree, and they don't come cheap.

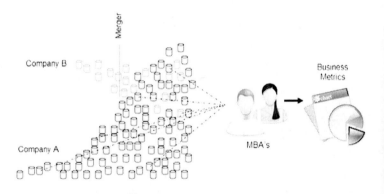

Figure 3: Analysts try to sort it out

The analysts will access the various systems, generate reports, and spend time trying to reconcile one system to the other. Given the complexity of the systems, the reports are never real-time – it takes time to pull reports and cross-check them over multiple systems.

Analysts may work to manually collect data and do primary analysis via Microsoft Excel® spreadsheets. However, maintaining a process so that results are consistent day to day and month to month is a challenge. If the analyst moves to another job, the new analyst may have different methods, and data consistency and process documentation are significant risk points to the company.

Even if the analyst has done their job, the reports may be fairly reliable, but conflicting data may force a judgment call – not a decision based on solid data. Finally, the metrics-gathering process is expensive when you account for the level of knowledge that is necessary and time it takes to build the intelligence. This is not optimal.

Don't get me wrong, there's nothing wrong with analysts. However, in big companies, analysts and those who otherwise manage data start to become pervasive throughout your organization. If you examine the company organizational chart and you have a large number of people who manage data for those who analyze data, it's a sure sign that data governance can help streamline your processes.

ETL and data warehouse

In the 1990s, another way that companies began solving this problem of siloed and widespread data was to create a data warehouse. The practice is to take nightly extracts of key data sources and build a process to extract, transform and load (ETL) business intelligence data into yet another database, so you'd have access to your metrics. This gave birth to companies like Informatica®, Ascential® (now part of IBM®), Teradata® and others. In fact, the data warehouse technologies worked, and still do work, to generate a central repository of data for business intelligence.

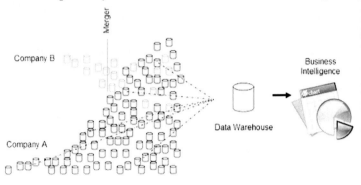

Figure 4: Data warehouse may be used

However, they have certain business shortcomings, such as:

- Require more resources, both in technology and expertise, to repeatedly extract big data sets and work out disparities between them;
- No easy process to load data back into source application;
- Source data remains disparate and managed by the rules of the individual business unit;
- Doesn't solve the problem of having to separately manage data silos with additional people;
- No centralized processes for improving data enterprise-wide;
- Business intelligence is rarely real-time.

Now I've talked with data warehouse experts who vehemently disagree with some or all of the above shortcomings. It's true that data warehouse vendors have dabbled in solving some of these issues. For example, if you have very fast hardware underneath your data warehouse, you can get near real-time business intelligence, with delays in minutes rather than days. However, the next evolution of data management calls for data governance, a centralized strategy for managing data across the enterprise that not only provides the metrics, but takes control of data for use throughout the company.

Building more efficiency

Beyond the simple business metrics, there are many questions you should be asking so that your company is running at the utmost efficiency. Questions like:

- Are we paying too much for that company we're buying or will adding their customer base to ours really increase revenue?
- Are we using our worldwide purchasing power to get the best deals and the greatest economy of scale from our suppliers?
- Do our executives trust the data, or are they relying more on gut instinct to make important decisions?
- When I send a mailing to the customer list or set of invoices, am I sure there is only one piece of mail for each customer, or does the customer get five copies? Are we being as ecologically friendly as possible?
- Do we trust the revenue numbers, or is our lack of provable correct revenue numbers subject to compliance issues? Are we in compliance with all laws regarding data management? Are any of our customers on the sanctions lists? Are any of our customers attempting to commit fraud on us?

Let's examine a few of these inefficiencies in detail.

The value of an acquisition

Mergers and acquisitions are an important part of doing business in this century. Particularly since the 1980s, mergers have been a very popular way to leapfrog the competition with new technologies, new markets and new customers.

In terms of buying a company for a new market or new customer list, it makes fiscal sense to buy other companies in your market to bring new customers into your fold. So, rather than paying for a marketing advertising campaign to get new customers, you can buy them as part of an acquisition. Because of this, most venture capitalists and business leaders know that two huge factors in determining a company's value during an acquisition are the customer and prospect lists.

However, it's strange how little the quality of the data assets and therefore their value is examined in the buy-out process. Before they buy, companies look at certain assets under a microscope – tangible assets like buildings and inventory are examined. Human assets, like the management staff are given a strong look. Cash flow is audited and examined with due diligence. But, data assets are often only given a hasty passing glance.

Data assets quickly dissolve when the company being acquired has data quality issues. It's not uncommon for a company to have 20%, 40%, or even 50% customer duplication (or near duplicates) in their database, for example. So, if you think you're getting 100,000 new customers, you may actually be getting 50,000 after you have cleansed the data. It's also common for actual inventory levels in the physical warehouse to be misaligned with the inventory levels in the enterprise resource planning (ERP) systems. This, too, may be due to data quality issues, and lead to surprises after the acquisition.

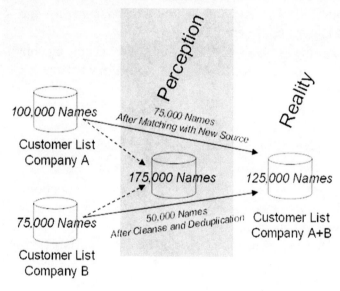

Figure 5: Data quality – perception v. reality

So what can you do as an acquiring company to mitigate these risks? The key is due diligence on data. Management must bring IT into the process as early as possible. IT must assess the data for post-acquisition costs like:

- Anomalies – missing data, near duplicates, and extraneous information all lead to additional costs when integrating data.

- Disparateness – having data spread out across multiple systems will cost the acquiring company extra time and money to integrate.
- Age – as data ages, its value decays. For name and address data, people move, die, get married, and get divorced frequently. For inventory data, parts become obsolete. The assessment should understand data age, if it is to be considered an asset.
- Overlap of data – does the data you're acquiring contain many matches for existing customers in your own database?
- Costs for data integration – the types of technologies used, how well they are documented and the quality of the data will affect the costs of data integration.

Data profiling technology, when used in conjunction with data governance methodologies, is a great way to understand most of these metrics. Today's data profiling and data discovery tools can analyze even the most obscure types of data and deliver metrics that talk to the value of the acquisition. By taking this extra step, you can reduce risk and understand the company you're buying. There's more about the technologies used in data governance later in this book.

Many of you may be thinking of the barriers that an acquiring company might face in getting accurate metrics about their acquisition. You certainly don't want to raise suspicion among stock holders, employees and the general public about your intention to acquire. You cannot make a business transaction like this in the public eye. When there are leaks, everyone and their opinions get involved and it becomes a complete stalemate. But that's what makes this a good job for a trusted internal data governance team, or a third-party consulting firm like Accenture®, Ernst & Young, Deloitte, and BT Global Services to name just a few. Before you buy, you should have a good understanding of a company's data assets, and a data governance program can help you establish that.

Decisions based on gut

Accenture's "Competing Through Business Analytics" survey interviewed about 250 US executives about how their companies use analytics to make decisions. A concurrent study of firms based in the United Kingdom found many similar results. According to the survey, 40% of major decisions are based on judgment rather than analytics. This represents a really amazing number of executives making "gut" decisions.

According to the survey, the reason for so many gut decisions is due to the lack of information. Most executives (61%) say that good data is not available. The Accenture survey also shows that company executives know they need to move away from making gut decisions – and move toward using real data to set decisions for business directions.

There is a growing understanding from c-level executives that high-performance companies use more than their gut feel to make decisions. For better decisions, data management strategies need to step up to meet goals based on analytics.

Data governance and being green

If you need another reason for data governance, it's all about being "green" today. It's clear that the green movement, specifically the desire for the general public to want to work with companies that are environmentally responsible, is here to stay.

The general public is overwhelmingly in favor of your efforts to be green. For example, Wal-Mart made headlines when it recently announced a program to reduce greenhouse gas emissions. Not only was this positive news for the world, but Wal-Mart saved money on reduced energy costs. In the case of Wal-Mart, they did things like installing skylights, which lowers lighting costs and saves resources. The announcement made for good public relations and an improvement to expenses – win/win.

Most green strategies are also aimed at improving business efficiencies as well as being great for the ecology. Whether it represents a concrete cost savings to heat your building with green technologies, for example, or if your customers are demanding green packaging, these are often business drivers.

For this and other reasons, marketers are relying less and less on ecologically unfriendly direct mail as a core channel to send targeted information to customers. Consumers' desire to be green are causing marketers and finance teams alike to rethink paper-based channels, increasing their reliance on electronic communications (e.g. websites, e-mail and e-statements). Direct mail is part of the strategy for marketing, but not the only one.

The green movement is changing the way we do business and the way we manage data as follows:

- **De facto name and address standards** – Being green is a serious subject to many of your customers. As we go forward, the general public simply won't accept duplicates. In the past, if you got three catalogs from that computer retailer, it was a joke. The public laughs no more and will use state mandated direct marketing laws to force you to take them off your list. Bills, marketing offers and other mailings from you must be as clean as possible, or you will risk the customer unsubscribing to your offers. If your company is reasonable and sends one catalog, you're more likely to maintain your permission to make future transactions with the customer.

- **Importance of non-name and address data** – Sure, the customer name and address will still be important, but additional information such as e-mail address, customer contact preferences, and whether the customer is on the "Do Not Call" list are fundamental. Build this type of data as you go forward with additional processes at the call center and sales level. In other words, if you want someone's e-mail address, you should ask for it.

- **Electronic billing** – As a customer, it sure is easier to get your bills via a website. As a company, it sure costs less to bill your customers via e-mail and secure website. As an eco-friendly company, it's a benefit to provide a way to stop all that paper from being delivered by the mailman. Electronic billing is a very convenient and valid strategy for your company to turn green. However, if your data is scattered across multiple systems, it will be extremely difficult to offer this convenience to your customers.

Data governance can help you meet these data management challenges and become greener. But if you consider the real impact of being green, it is equally about customer satisfaction as it is about some philanthropic corporate goal.

Improving compliance with BASEL II and SOX

Flawed data introduces regulatory risks for your company. In Europe, BASEL II is standard operating procedure at many financial services companies and the US is starting to come in line. BASEL II is complex, but includes mandates for increased transparency of key performance indicators. Financial institutions must know such things as probability of default (PD) and exposure at default (EAD) to better understand their risk. BASEL II has strict rules on a company's capital risks and forces you to reserve capital to avoid penalties. You must provide correct analysis of your risk position or become subject to fines.

To comply with BASEL II, financial services have to be smarter than ever in managing data. Data feeds into your risk calculation models. For example, let's say you're a bank and you're calculating the risk of your debtors. You enrich your data with Standard & Poor's ratings to understand the risk. But if the data is non-standardized, you may have a hard time matching the Standard & Poor's data to your customer. If not found, a company with a AA- bond rating might default as BB- in the database. After all, it is wise to be conservative if you don't know the risk. But those types of errors can cause thousands, even millions to be set unnecessarily aside. These additional capital reserves can be a major drag on the company.

Unaddressed issues can cause your company not only to receive penalties for noncompliance, but may have other financial implications, too. With the proper data you can fix the risk-rating process by establishing data governance. When you work on key data attributes and set up rules to ensure the accuracy of data, a financial services company will save money.

The Sarbanes-Oxley Act is a piece of legislation from the United States that has had an impact on the way we manage data. The Act contains eleven sections, ranging from some additional corporate board responsibilities to criminal penalties for non-compliance. Section 3 of the act mandates that senior executives take individual responsibility for the accuracy and completeness of corporate financial reports. Section 4, among other things, requires internal controls for assuring the accuracy of financial reports and disclosures, and requires audits on those controls. In order to accomplish compliance with this Act, you have to manage your data. Corporate officers have to trust that the data quality is accurate or risk the possibility of fines or jail sentences. The best way to do that is by using data profiling tools, using them to set up checks and balances on your data and ensuring the accuracy of your financial reports.

Designated terrorist organizations

Another common compliance issue that mandates data governance has to do with the lists of terrorists offered by the European Union, Australia, Canada and the United States. For example, in the United States, the US Treasury Department publishes a list of terrorists and narcotics traffickers. These individuals and companies are called "Specially Designated Nationals" or SDNs. Their assets are blocked and companies in the United States are prohibited from dealing with them. In the United Kingdom, the Bank of England maintains a separate list.

If your company fails to identify and block a target account (of a terrorist, for example), there could be real world consequences such as a transfer of funds or other valuable property to an SDN, an enforcement action against your bank or company, and negative publicity. On the other hand, many cases may be a false positive, where the name is similar to a target's name, but the rest of the information provided by the applicant does not match the descriptor information on the SDN list. The false positives can cause embarrassment and poor customer relationships.

A data governance program can help you both correctly identify foreign nationals on the SDN list and lower the number of false positives. If the data coming into your system is standardized and has all of the required information as mandated by your governance program, matching technologies and automatically identifying SDNs can be more easily accomplished.

Why data governance?

So it is for all of these issues that companies find themselves in need of data governance. Data governance heralds the maturation of a company from a small business into an enterprise. Data governance can be a remedy for information availability issues, customer dissatisfaction, and inefficient supply and procurement systems. Data governance provides the long-term strategy to solve accounting and billing issues, and it can save your company thousands as your industry's laws change. You just need a data management strategy, called "data governance," to make it all happen.

Who needs data governance?

The short answer is that every organization, regardless of size or type of business could benefit from some form of data governance. If you agree with the basic concept that sound business decisions cannot be based on inaccurate or incomplete data, then you should agree that data governance is an important strategy for your business. If you make decisions based on gut feel, you are clearly gambling with the future of your company. Every organization must pay attention to data management in order to understand its business, provide maximum profit and efficiency, and be confident in its decisions.

CHAPTER 2: WHAT IS DATA GOVERNANCE?

To start with, data governance is a set of processes that ensures that important data assets are formally managed throughout the enterprise. Data governance guarantees that data can be trusted and that people can be made accountable for any adverse event that happens because of poor data quality. It is about putting people in charge of fixing and preventing issues with data, so that the enterprise can become more efficient.

Data governance also describes an evolutionary process for a company, altering the company's way of thinking and setting up the processes to handle information, so that it may give power and intelligence to the entire organization. It's about using technology when necessary in many forms to help aid the process. When companies desire, or are required, to gain control of their data, they empower their people, set up processes and get help from technology to do it.

How do different groups see data governance?

Cross-functional perspectives on data governance may vary. From an organization perspective, data governance is like the elephant in a dark room. If you feel its tail, it's a snake. If you touch his leg, it feels like a tree. It's a matter of perspective for the type of employee who may be looking at data governance.

For a CEO and other c-level executives, data governance is about getting efficiency into the organization, getting the most out of your knowledge workers and making sure your people get the metrics they need to make good decisions. Upper management knows that if you can't get the information you need, you can't make good business decisions. C-level executives are also becoming more and more aware of regulations. Having a solid data management strategy means to them that they will do their job in keeping the company from running afoul of the law by being able to generate accurate financial reports.

For business users, data governance is about their enterprise and desktop applications and the data behind them. There may be some doubt behind the information they're getting from their systems. The new customer relationship management (CRM) system, for example, may not be meeting expectations, not because of the application itself, but because of the data behind it. Business users may struggle with this and even want to help. It's a good thing they do, because part of the charter of data governance is to bring business users into the process to help.

Business users also need to know that they are part of the challenge when it comes to data governance. For example, if you sloppily enter data into the CRM system, the results of sales and marketing programs will become sloppy. In other words, if you put garbage in, you'll get garbage out. Business users need to understand that data quality is everyone's job and not just an issue with technology.

For IT staff, data governance is about setting up master data management platforms, understanding what data is available, gaining access to the data, cleansing and standardizing, and managing metadata models for the utmost efficiency. For technologists, they are looking for a way to improve the quality of the data that is causing so many problems for the users they support.

The more technical among us will often talk about data governance in terms of data modeling. In this book, I will not delve too deeply into this rabbit hole. Like *Alice's Adventures in Wonderland*, this rabbit hole contains an absurd and improbable world inhabited by many strange characters. However, from a thirty-thousand-foot view, data modeling allows you to establish corporate-wide (or maybe just a project-wide) standards for data. It lets technologists define which fields exist in any given database and what should be contained in each field. The models are commonly used in data warehouse and business intelligence applications. When data models are enforced, information quality benefits. Data models are also a key component of master data management (MDM) technology.

Broken data model example

As a member of the data governance team, your role may not include the requirement to know how to formulate a data model. However, you should know that data models, if done properly, specify the rules for any given database table. You need to understand the impact of data models, how they get broken and why they get broken. There are many stories where a broken data model caused strange issues with the data.

One good example of a broken data model was a project we encountered at Trillium Software, while we cleansed the data set of a major utility company. The company was consolidating disparate meter readers' data into a centralized repository of customers. The data was to be used in marketing and billing as part of a new customer relationship management system. But as the company consolidated the data, spurious characters would appear in the data, such as:

- `John Smith LDIY`
  `22 Elm St.`
  `Dedham, MA 02026`

In another record:

- `Judy Johnson`
  `44 Main St. L D I Y`
  `Dedham, MA 02026`

Yet another record:

- `Frank Brown`
  `23 Oak Ave`
  `L.D.I.Y. Dedham, MA 02026`

The random characters inserted in the addresses were sure to cause problems with bills and their ability to be delivered by the post office. The first temptation was to simply strip out the extra characters. Wisely, the technologists did not.

After making some calls to the manager that led the meter readers, the data governance team determined that LDIY was a meter-reading acronym meaning "Large Dog In Yard" and that the meter readers were inserting this very valuable information to warn of the danger of dogs. By not having the proper data structure to store this information, meter readers were forced to break the rules of the data model and insert it where they could.

Breaking the data model is common and this example shows that it's a very good idea for business users to work with technologists to fix the data model. The data model is broken because only address information should be stored in an address field, not warnings about pets with teeth. Clearly there should have been a better way to store the LDIY data. Those definitions can be turned into an improved data model by technologists. In this case, the data model needed to have a place to insert meter reading instructions like "LDIY" and "Meter on Right".

People break data models for several reasons. When the systems are old and inflexible, users may be forced to enter data into fields that aren't meant to hold it. The database manager may be inexperienced or indifferent and recommend breaking the data model to save themself time and configuration work. Of course, this usually means that someone will have to fix an even bigger mess later down the line.

When you break the rules of a data model, it has a huge impact on your ability to do data governance. Let's say, for example, rather than setting up a new table in the database, a programmer who worked for you in the past used 99/99/9999 in a date field to designate an inactive account; it is a quick fix that is all too common and even recommended in some of the programming manuals of yesterday. To deal with it, the database programmer had to customize the database and application and write some business rules so that the application did what it was supposed to do.

It all works fine when the data is used within the single application. However, these sorts of shortcuts cause huge headaches for the data governance team as they try to consolidate and move data from silo to enterprise-wide.

They first must realize that some dates contain all 9s – one of the advantages of using data profiling tools in the beginning of the process. Second, they must figure out what the 9s mean by meeting with members of the business community. Hopefully, someone from that era still works for the company so that they can determine that. Finally, they must plan to migrate that data over to a data model that makes more sense, like having an active/inactive account table.

If you take that one example and amplify it across thousands of tables in your company, you'll get a good understanding of the importance of maintaining and enforcing the rules designated by data models.

For the purposes of this book, that's about as deep as I'll go into data modeling wonderland. If this is something you want to understand more completely, pick up one of the books by Dr Ralph Kimball; I would recommend *The Data Warehouse Toolkit: The Complete Guide to Dimensional Modeling*. Dr Kimball is perhaps the best-known and respected author in this area.

Defining data governance by its benefits

Given the varying perspectives on what data governance is, you can see why the definition varies, depending upon who you ask. But let's consider another angle – you can also define data governance by what it offers to the organization.

Fewer adverse events

A goal of data governance is to have fewer negative events as a result of poor data. Poor information quality can begin to lead to adverse events both inside and outside the walls of the company, even though they are seemingly unrelated events. For example:

- Marketing becomes counterproductive. Marketing may be inadvertently barraging certain customers with multiple mailers leading to loss of customers. The data may contain duplicates and near-duplicates that are showing up on your customers' doorstep as bundles of junk mail. The barrage causes lower marketing effectiveness and customer apathy.
- Inability to ship products on time due to incorrect inventory levels. The data for the inventory is unstructured and not standardized. Inventory levels for certain items may be inappropriate – too high and you're stuck with extra inventory. Too low and you're not able to deliver products/service on time.
- Bad guys taking advantage of your company's free give-aways. In an attempt to defraud the company, customers may give slightly different versions of their name and address to receive free giveaways. The give-aways might have been effective if you could hold them to one per customer, but less effective when people cheat. This is costly for the corporation and only works to create even more poor data.
- Your company buys equipment that you already have in inventory. Because of the data inconsistencies, a simple equipment check showed no available transformers, which appeared in the system as "trnsfmr." Spending money when you don't have to is bad enough.

Hopefully, the equipment in inventory won't expire before you use it.

- The company is in a bidding war with some unnamed competitor and must drop its price significantly to win the business. After the bidding is done, the company learns that it was actually bidding against itself – the British division bidding against the French division. Because of lack of a unified sales and territory system, the company loses significant revenue.

- The IT team spends millions on a new ERP or CRM system. However, because of poor data governance and poor data quality, the system is unusable. Business users can't get the information they need and lose faith in the value of the IT team.

- Inaccurate billing indicates false revenue. Earnings reconciled after all the customer complaints have been filed might indicate a very different revenue number than any number that was predicted by the analysts. Data governance may help avoid negative stockholder reaction to earnings falling short of estimates.

- Lack of understanding of your biggest customer causes you to lose that customer.

We've only scratched the surface – the list of potential adverse events is unending. The good news is that if you are thinking about or embarking on a data governance initiative, these lemons are perfectly ripe and ready to make lemonade. You can point to these same events as you begin your data governance initiative and begin to ask for more resources to solve them.

Building the IT–business bridge

A goal and benefit of data governance that should not be overlooked is that data governance is about business users and technologists working together to have fewer adverse events. Business users and executives know what information they need to make the business successful. Technologists know to some degree what metrics the data can provide. In between, there is a disconnect in many organizations.

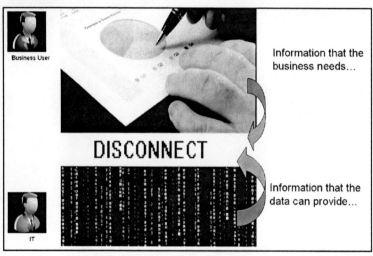

Figure 6: Business–IT disconnect

To further the disconnect, technologist users tend to use the language of technology – terabytes, metadata management, and look-up tables – while business users tend to use the language of business – return on investment, cost per click, inventory costs. That's why data governance is about communication between business and IT, identifying a common language, and meeting the needs of the organization.

It's the new data governance team, headed up by titles like "Director of Information" and "Enterprise Data Governance Facilitator" that make the difference in data governance. They dare to attempt to bridge the gap between what the business needs to thrive, against the data that exists in the enterprise systems. Often the data has shortcomings, which must be identified and, if need be, addressed by a data governance team.

CHAPTER 3: DEFINING DATA GOVERNANCE SUCCESS

An important concept that must be defined early in a data governance process is how to exactly define success. Since we've defined data governance as process improvements to better manage data, success would dovetail into creating an organizational structure that oversees the corporate use of data and makes life better for everyone in the organization.

However, every company is a little different. There will likely be generic success factors that almost every company will need to measure. There will also be very specific factors that only companies that share your industry or history will have in common with you.

That's not to say that the definition of success must remain some sort of a corporate dogma. The definition of success will change as your data governance initiative marches on. Initially, most companies set the bar fairly low and still realize huge benefits from small improvements. As you begin to deliver better and better information to the business, they will begin to believe in data governance and tend to demand more from you. So, the doctrine must evolve as your company's collective data governance IQ evolves.

Generic data governance success factors

While it's true that your company will have a unique reference and be at a different evolutionary position than any other company, there are the success factors that almost every company will share in order to achieve success. These include the following:

Fix data anomalies

A data anomaly is any data that is unsuitable for the intended use because it doesn't conform to project standards. Here are some typical anomalies you may uncover as you look into your data:

- non-numeric data going into a numeric field;
- unexpected values embedded within data;
- missing or incomplete data;
- misfielded data;
- comma-reversed names;
- data that doesn't follow a prescribed format, for example, part number 459-234 does not follow xx-xxx format;
- fields that should be unique that aren't, as in the case of a primary key.

To discover anomalies, data governance teams will generally perform data quality profiling. The profiling will in turn translate into important data quality metrics. The Total Data Quality Management (TDQM) Research Program at the Massachusetts Institute of Technology accurately describes the anomalies you find in data might include accuracy, timeliness, precision, reliability, currency, completeness and relevancy. No matter what issues get in the way, fixing data anomalies and keeping them fixed, is definitely the primary goal of a data governance program.

Develop a repeatable process

From day one, data governance teams need to begin to develop a unified process to obtain reliable, accurate data to use in various circumstances simultaneously today and to re-use tomorrow. You should begin to document a process for solving information quality problems in a way that builds a foundation for meeting tomorrow's challenges with the same efficiencies that were used to solve the data problems of today's project.

You will find that your first data quality initiative leads to a better corporate understanding of the business information available and the possibilities for connecting it to other information.

For example, your company may collect customer data from various business units, including sales, web, call centers and accounting. Each of these business functions might have different information about your customers since each function has a different way of doing business. Some records have information, others lack complete contact information; some have information that is more up-to-date than others. Building a flexible process and technology solution that you can leverage in other data silos is also a long-term goal.

Most data governance efforts start out as a single project with the understanding that the process must grow and extend over time to support multiple applications. We're often cautioned about "boiling the ocean" when it comes to data governance. Your job is to start with limited scope projects, while fostering a culture shift that spreads like a computer virus through your organization. Data governance will eventually become part of every new project.

Handle change

Corporate change, such as rapid growth, mergers, downsizing and new laws governing the corporation, happens frequently in business. Part of the data governance team's mission is to allow the company to handle change more easily. To do that, data governance teams must:

- provide stability in repeatable processes and outcomes for data management;
- document the processes and solutions they use;
- communicate the plans for change with the entire business;
- choose solutions and processes that can handle change.

To negate the effect of employee turnover and other types of changes, some organizations turn to third-party consulting services to help document and provide continuity. It's a solid strategy to protect against organizational change.

Coordinate efforts with business

The power of data governance is found in many different business initiatives. Yet, the power of the data can often only be understood by the business users that use it.

In our LDIY example above, the technologists easily could have disposed of the extraneous characters during the cleansing process. But they didn't. Instead, a meeting with the meter readers revealed a jewel hidden in the data. Having information about on-the-job trouble spots could go on to affect employee attrition rates and even workers' compensation claims.

Success comes when you can deliver the right information to the right people in the organization. It's impossible to tell what the right data is, unless you coordinate efforts with those who use it.

Data ownership

Data governance flies in the face of traditional data management practices from a corporate politics point of view. Traditionally the silos of data are owned by a particular business unit or organization. Sometimes the business units are even competing with each other for revenue and resources within the parent company. Data governance teams must strike a political balance among competing goals. An understanding of the boundaries of departmental versus enterprise data ownership must be communicated. Any disagreements must go to the quick decision of an executive, who can mandate policies and change.

On the other hand, there are some organizations where nobody owns the data. This, too, can lead to problems. When something goes wrong as the data is used, or if the data is used irresponsibly, nobody is accountable and no one is responsible for the harm the data may have caused to the reputation of the organization. Data governance assigns data ownership and makes the data governance team responsible.

An example of this made the news in May of 2007, when a contractor for IBM lost multiple data tapes while transporting them between facilities. According to the *InformationWeek* article, the tapes contained information on IBM employees, those who were still working for the company, along with retirees, people who left for other jobs, and people who might have left the company and then returned. The tapes held personal information on them, including names, addresses, birth dates, Social Security numbers, and beginning and end dates of employment. As a former IBM employee, I myself was contacted by IBM who acted quickly to clean up the mess. With fear of litigation looming, the company sprung for a credit watch service for myself and other IBM employees. The mess may have been avoided if accountability was assigned to the data and a process for securing data was clearly thought out.

Specific data governance success

So, if goals like 1) fixing data anomalies; 2) establishing repeatable processes; 3) being able to handle change effectively; 4) coordinating data management with business; and, 5) taking ownership of the data are not enough, many companies will have additional corporate goals around data governance. You will take a closer look at those goals as you begin to seek the highest impact project and establish synergies between technologists and business.

Success in data governance is often as unique as the organization itself. A marketing organization will define success in its ability to reach customers effectively, making contact information important. A major retailer would likely define success in its ability to manage the supply chain and vendor partnerships. Financial services companies would likely look toward compliance as the primary measure of success.

Organization-specific success should always be measured in terms of ROI, and that is the topic that I'll cover in Chapter 4.

CHAPTER 4: GETTING FUNDED FOR IQ PROJECTS

Knowing all this about the value of data and the power of data governance, there are probably some of you nodding your heads and who are ready to take on making positive changes in your organization. If you are beginning to become enthusiastic about the power of data, you are discovering your inner data champion. That's good, because the responsibility for getting funded and initiating data governance heavily falls on the shoulders of the data champion.

You may just be a data governance champion if you're ready to start right now on the data governance initiative. However, there is that issue of funding and resources that you have to overcome. You may be convinced, but the folks who approve purchase orders are not yet impressed.

Let's take a look at this critical role, as it is important to getting funded for data governance and information quality projects.

The data champion

A data champion is someone who is the glue between business, IT and third-party providers. Champions are passionate about data governance and promote its benefit to all whom they meet. They are the vision of data governance, developing new efficient processes and working through any issues of non-cooperation that arise.

Since a data champion is so important, let's take a look at some traits that are required to be effective in this role.

Knowledge

The data champion role requires someone who has both technology and business knowledge – someone who can communicate with others and build relationships as needed. In a way, a data champion is a translator, translating the technologist's jargon of schemas and metadata into business value, and vice versa. To do that, you really need to understand what makes both sides tick.

Develop cross-functional relationships

A successful data champion is usually someone who can develop cross-functional relationships. Data in your organization generally belongs to someone, often a division that is owned and managed by someone other than you. As you begin to implement data governance, you will have to work with different types of personalities across the organization.

In fact, you may find it helpful to create a list of the key stakeholders, their supervisors, their data sources. A data champion should be willing to reach out to them and to evangelize data governance.

It is not easy to create and maintain relationships. If you're particularly bad at this, there are several good books on how to do this well. One of my favorites is Dale Carnegie's *How to Win Friends and Influence People*. This king of all people-skills books was first published in 1937 and still remains the best book of its kind to lead you to success.

Dale Carnegie training programs are also available in most major cities across the globe. I have personally taken some of the courses and have received great benefit from them. I have never met a fellow Dale Carnegie graduate who has told me otherwise. The course entitled "Effective Communications and Human Relations" is a great place to start.

Selling the vision

One of the success traits of a good data champion is that they have vision and they can sell it. The vision may not necessarily come from one person. Working with others within your organization to develop a vision is important. However, the data champion may be the primary voice of the vision.

Successful data champions use the power of the elevator pitch to promote the data governance vision to all who will listen. The term elevator pitch describes a sales message that can be delivered in the time span of an elevator ride. The pitch should have a clear, consistent message and reflects your goals to make the company more efficient through data governance. The more effective the speech, the more interested your colleagues will become. They'll want to know more.

So, the next time someone asks you "How's it going?" or "What are you working on these days?" be ready with your pitch. You can give these speeches in the elevator, at the water bubbler and at lunch. You should try to customize your pitch to show how your vision can have a direct impact on the person you're talking to. If you're talking to someone in finance, talk about how data governance can make for a more efficient billing process. If you're talking to someone in marketing, talk about more efficient marketing campaigns. Know your audience and speak to it.

Employee: What's up, Greg?

Data Champion: What's up? We're busy saving the company a bundle of money, that's what's up.

Employee: What, are they planning to take away free morning coffee now?

Data Champion: No, we're working through some issues with marketing. They've been mailing out promotion and have been getting tons of undeliverable mail back. Did you know that those pieces cost about $2 each to send? We found 20,000 duplicate names and about 10,000 completely invalid addresses. Let's see, that's...thirty times two...$60,000 per mailing. Not bad. Only the tip of the iceberg...We're tackling billing data next.

Employee: Wow. Impressive.

Data Champion: It's all about the data, my friend. All about the data...

Being positive

Most importantly, a data champion must smile and train himself to think positively. Why? Positive thinking is contagious and your optimism will build positive energy for your project. Smile and speak optimistically to give others the confidence to agree with you.

You will encounter negative people who will attempt to set up road blocks in front of you. But you have to be patient and pragmatic. As long as you're optimistic and positive, you will be a very successful data champion. Those who join you on your quest will also share in the same success.

Leadership

A data champion is a leader above all, so studying the qualities of successful leaders will serve you well. Before you begin to champion the cause of data governance, you'll want to become a student of leadership. This will help you overcome objections and inspire the data governance team.

In *The 21 Indispensable Qualities of a Leader*, author John Maxwell identifies the top traits such as character, charisma, commitment, communication, competence, vision and others. Many find this book to be a valuable resource in their career development. It will help you in leading the team.

Return on investment

We've talked a lot about you, but let's look at your organization's requirements. All successful companies are looking for an investment, not an expense. Before spending money on data quality improvements, executives and business stakeholders will ask you for a business case that demonstrates the value of your project to the organization. Showing the hard numbers and benefit is often the only way to get funded for information quality projects. In turn, having successful information quality projects leads to maturation of the company in terms of data governance.

Your manager may ask you for a cost justification for a data governance initiative. *Even if it's not required, prepare one.* Quantifying the impact of data governance will show the value you are providing to your organization and will establish a tangible return on investment (ROI). Later, you can point to this ROI when you ask for future investments in data governance.

Building a business case first must take into consideration corporate information and the relationship it has on business processes. It further considers the relationship between those processes and business results. Simply put, there are three primary areas for business impact:

- increasing revenue
- lowering costs
- reducing risks (compliance).

Your purchase order approvers don't care about nulls or metadata. They simply want to know how the project impacts these three things.

Picking the right projects

It's difficult to win at the data governance game if you pick projects that have limited upside. That is why picking the right projects to start your data governance initiative is so important. Your tendency might be to fix the data of the business users who are complaining the most or those that the CEO tells you to fix.

While the IT staff is busy working its way through the complaints, prospecting for more to do is somewhat counter-intuitive. At the onset, you may feel like you have quite enough to do. Fact is, it's only these high-value projects that will get you noticed by management and propel your team into a position of higher prominence. It really comes down to the fact that in IT there are two types of projects you can be a part of:

- **Squeaky wheel projects** – ones that keep things running the way they should run. Examples of squeaky wheels include upgrading servers with more storage, installing the latest version of software so that the company doesn't de-support it, adding a new table in a database, etc.
- **Nitrous oxide projects** – nitrous oxide is used by racers to boost the horse power of their cars. Nitrous oxide projects are ones that add a big boost to your organization, making it run faster and better than the competition. Data governance is an example of a nitrous oxide project because the potential cost savings to a company can be millions of dollars/pounds/euros and can boost your company beyond its current operating speed.

In order to achieve greatness within the organization, your team must both oil the squeaky wheel and install the nitrous. However untrue, the organization's view of squeaky wheel projects are negative, either because the inconvenience they cause, limited business value, or expectation that someone should have thought of that already. From the corporate view, you should have anticipated that we'd need more storage or that we needed that table in the database. Greasing the squeaks is necessary to maintain the status quo, but rarely are they seen as innovative.

When you begin picking high-value targets with huge upside potential, the nitrous oxide projects, you'll begin to win at the data governance game. People will stand up and notice when you begin to bring in the higher qualifying times. You'll get better traction in the organization and be able to think about adding a roll bar, new wheels and turbo charger. (There's only one more car metaphor to go, so hang in there.) The additional velocity you provide to the organization can make it easier for you as you take on new challenges.

Building credibility

So, if building credibility is the key to overcoming the resistance, how do we gain credibility? One of the easiest ways is to start to form relationships. If you were to sit down and work for a day in the billing center, call center or purchasing agent job, for example, people there will see that you understand them and care about their processes. Walk a mile in their shoes. Feel their pain. At the very least, you could invite a business person to lunch to understand their challenges. The hearts and minds of the people can be won in this manner. The first, most important task you can do is to understand critical business processes in your organization.

Leveraging a crisis

A data governance champion will always be on the look-out for a crisis caused by lack of data management and lack of enterprise standards. They will know how to stand up and point out the information quality problem behind the crisis without becoming overly annoying. The champion educates and offers positive solutions to a crisis – the solution being data governance.

So, keep your eyes open for a marketing mailing that goes wrong, problems in manufacturing, and executives that make bad decisions based on gut feel rather than hard metrics. After all, a good leader, like your boss, would probably make better decisions if the information was trustworthy.

Leveraging new initiatives

A data governance champion will be on the lookout for new data intensive projects. The list might include the upgrade of a customer relationship management system, a new data warehouse, consolidation of systems, or just about any situation where large amounts of data must be moved. These new initiatives are optimal when a division of work is assigned, like an applications team to handle the software and the data governance team to handle the data migration.

Conversation starters

Let's say you've heard a rumor that marketing is having problems contacting their customers or that your buyer is having some frustration with the enterprise resource planning (ERP) system. It sounds like a data problem to you, but how do you start the conversation?

Below is a table of conversation starters you might use to begin to peel back the layers of the onion and understand your business value.

| **Marketing** | Have you been working on any new campaigns? |
| | How are your list(s)? |

What kind of return rate do you get on those mailings?

How's the CRM system working out for you?

Do you think we have the data to foster strong relationships with our customers?

Procurement

Does the data always reflect the correct inventory?

Have you ever paid a vendor twice for the same item?

Do our prices for the items we buy reflect our global buying power?

Has anything ever been done to try to prevent this? Why do you think it didn't work?

Supply chain

Do our shipments ever get returned? What are the costs of that?

If we had a product recall, how effective would we be in reaching our customers?

How do you deal with keeping inventory costs low despite duplicate parts in the database?

Do we share our product availability with any partners? How's that going?

Executive

Do you get the metrics you need to make decisions? Do you trust the revenue numbers you get? Have they ever been wrong?

Do you wish you had more reliable metrics?

	How confident are you that we are in compliance with all laws in our country and the countries in which we do business?
Billing	Do we overbill or underbill our customers?
	Do invoices reach our customers properly, or are some of them lost/returned?

You may find these questions useful as you begin to prospect for new projects and quantify return on investment.

The four whys

The questions I've outlined here may be followed by what's known as the "four whys," a practice that states that you have to ask why four times in order to get to the root of the problem.

Example: Do the company's shipments ever get returned?

Answer: Yes, occasionally we see that. Last year, we were penalized by our shipping company for over $30K per quarter. I wish there was something we could do about it.

First why: Why do you think they get returned?

Answer: The address is bad. Most of our sales guys are sloppy typers.

Second why: Don't they have software to check addresses now? Why don't we use something like that?

Answer: The system doesn't check the addresses in real time. I think there's a data warehouse process that does it, but only after the nightly update. Meanwhile the shipment is already gone.

Third why: Why do you think sales guys get sloppy about the data? Why isn't there a check in real time?

Answer: The sales guys are in a hurry and they don't understand the impact it has. I guess a solution that does real-time address checking would help, too. Every time I bring it up, the boss says it's too expensive.

Fourth why: What happens when a shipment comes back?

Answer: Well, we have a process for returned shipments. It's Nigel's job in shipping to process the returns and follow-up with the sales guys on the correct address. If the sales rep isn't available, he might go to accounting or contracts to rustle up the correct address. He also notifies the customer and customer service that the shipment is delayed. He has thick skin since customers can really lean on him when that happens.

Obviously I didn't start every question with a "why," but you get the idea. The example is here to illustrate a point. By asking "why" four times, we've developed a map directly to the root of the problem and uncovered some processes to improve along the way.

Return on investment

Once the research is underway, you can begin to build some spreadsheets that capture the potential return on investment (ROI). The intent is to document the most impactful data quality problems and then enumerate all the costs incurred by each of those issues.

An ROI calculation must compare the costs associated with the improvements to the financial gain possible by the improvement. Therefore, data governance teams need to look at the specific problems that are the root causes and what it would cost to fix those problems.

From our four-whys conversation, you learned some interesting facts. Now take your information and put it into a statement about ROI.

Problem
The entry of erroneous data into the CRM system causes shipping penalties of $30,000 per quarter and other losses due to inefficiency. Human resources devote a full time employee to mitigate the problem.
Annual impact
Shipping penalties and re-ship costs – $120,000 ($30,000 per quarter) Man Hours – $100,000 per year
Solutions
Sales training ($5000) Real-time address checking ($50,000)
Impact
Reduce shipping penalties by 50% in first year. Further reductions in subsequent years. Decreasing follow-up work for Nigel by 50%. Gives Nigel time to assist in manufacturing.

Return on investment	
Year 1 costs: $55,000	Year 1 savings: Shipping penalties: $60,000 Man hours: $50,000 TOTAL: $110,000
Year 1 ROI: $55,000	
Year 2 costs: $27,500 (License Costs)	Year 2 savings: Shipping penalties: $75,000 Man hours: $60,000 TOTAL: $135,000
Year 2 ROI: $107,500	
Options	
Keep status quo: Continue annual costs of $220,000 Continual increase in customer dissatisfaction.	

If you don't know how to calculate man hours, talk to accounting or human resources. Chances are, your company has a figure for average weighted salary costs, which takes into account salary plus payroll taxes, insurance, vacation pay, holiday pay, sick pay, and all the other expenses of an employee. If there are people who are working on a task that can be automated, those human resources can go to another part of the organization in need.

The "do nothing" option

I'm going to point out the last two lines of the above statement. It's very important to remember the "do nothing" option, something learned from the data governance team at a major telecommunications company with a very successful data governance implementation. Always calculate what will happen if you do nothing about the data quality – the "do nothing" option. Sounds simple, but it's very powerful. In your scoping and ROI documents, make sure that you state in black and white both the ROI of improving data quality processes and the potential risks that you run when you ignore it. In short, if you invest resources in information quality, all will be right with the world. If you do nothing, anarchy, chaos and excessive costs will surely ensue.

These types of proposals tend to meet with greater success than any form of technical proposal. Avoid telling the business about your database schemas, metadata management or probabilistic matching techniques. While they may be significant parts of the project, they won't get you the money you need to start the project.

Overcoming objections to data governance

You've created a wonderful proposal. You've brought it up to management, but the chiefs tell you there's just no budget for data governance. Now what?

Keep at it. Rome wasn't built in a day and neither is data governance. You know that data governance is the right thing to do for both your team and your company. You know that any money spent on data governance will usually come back with multipliers. It just may take some time for others to get on board. Be patient and continue your quest. Meanwhile, here are some ideas to continue to try:

Corporate revenue

Today, companies manage spending tightly, looking at the expenses and revenue each fiscal quarter and each month to optimize the all-important operating income (revenue minus expenses equals operating income). If sales and revenue are weak, management gets miserly. On the other hand, if revenue is high and expenses are low, your high-ROI proposal will have a better chance for approval.

For many people I know, this corporate reality is hard to deal with. Logical thinkers would suggest that if something is broken, it should be fixed, no matter how well the sales team is performing. The people who run your business have their first priorities set on stockholder value. You, too, should pay attention to your company's sales figures as they are announced each quarter. If your company has a quarterly revenue call, use it to strike when the environment for spending is right.

Cheap wins

If there is no money to spend on information quality, there still may be potential for information quality wins for you to exploit. For example, let's say you were to profile or make some SQL queries into your company's supply chain system database and you found a part that has a near duplicate. So, part number "21-998 Condenser" and part number "2-1-998 Cndsr" exist as duplicated parts in your supply chain.

After verifying the fairly obvious duplicate, you can ask your friend on the procurement side how much it costs to store and hold these condensers in inventory. Then use some guerilla marketing techniques to extol the virtues of data governance. After all, if you could find this with just SQL queries, consider how much you could find with a data discovery/profiling tool. Better yet, consider how much you could find with a company-wide initiative.

Case studies

Case studies are a great way to spread the word about data governance. They usually contain real-world examples, often of your competitors, who are finding gold with better attention to information quality. Vendors in the data governance space will have case studies on their websites, or you can get unpublished studies by asking your sales representative.

I once co-presented a data governance case study in conjunction with a data champion from a major manufacturer of office printers. The presentation was delivered at a local SAP-focused conference. Shortly after my presentation, I was approached by one of the manufacturer's competitors who knew he could internally sell data management after hearing that his competitor does it and that it brings great benefit. My point is, consider that built-in desire of your company to be competitive, and keep your Google searches and alerts tuned to what data management projects are underway at your competitors.

Industry analysts will also do case studies. Gartner Research also has non-biased case studies on some of the biggest implementations of data governance in the world. If you are a Gartner customer, it's a good place to start.

Analysts

While I'm on the subject of analysts, they are another valuable source for proving your point about the virtues of data governance. Your boss may have installed his own custom spam filter against your cajoling on data governance. But he doesn't have to take your word for it; he can listen to an industry expert.

If you own a subscription to an analyst firm, use it to sell the power of data governance. Analysts offer telephone consultations, reports and webinars to clients. These offerings may be useful to sway your team.

The analyst firm Aberdeen does research on industry trends. They generally start a research project with a poll on a certain emerging topic and ask companies that are similar to yours what they are doing and what they are planning. This type of research may be compelling to your management, since it provides statistics on the actions of best-in-class companies.

Firms like Gartner Research, Current Analysis, Bloor Research and Forrester are more focused on having a single analyst researching a particular topic. That research may take the form of vendor meetings, meetings with implementers of data governance, industry events and other forms of research. The analysts become very knowledgeable on the topic and become the central aggregator on trends in the market. The findings often make their way into reports published by the analyst. If you're a client, you can download them and/or talk to the analyst to understand a certain aspect of data governance.

If you are not a client of these firms, go to the data governance vendors again. If there is a crucial report, they will often license it to offer on their website for download, particularly if it speaks well about their solution.

Data governance expert sessions

This technique also falls within the category of "don't just take my word for it." An increasing number of data governance practitioners, including solution vendors and consultants, have developed some very compelling presentation materials on how data governance can help your organization.

You can find a data governance workshop to assist your organization with developing your data quality strategies. Often conducted for a group, the session leader interacts with a group of your choosing and presents the potential for improving the efficiency of your business with data governance. As the meeting leader, you would invite both technologists and business users. Include those who are skeptical of the value a data-quality program will bring to their company; a third-party opinion may sway them. The cost is usually reasonable or free and it can help the group understand and share key concepts of data governance.

This is a service offered by The Data Governance Institute, Baseline Consulting, Trillium Software, Accenture, BT and many others.

Guerilla marketing

Why not start your own personal crusade, your own marketing initiative to drive home the power of information quality? In my data governance blog, I offer graphics for use in your signature file to drive home the importance of IQ to your organization. Use the power of a newsletter, blog, or e-mail signature to get your message across.

An example is this banner:

Figure 7: Getting your message across

(*http://data-governance.blogspot.com/2009/01/starting-your-own-personal-data-quality.html*)

Clearly, the banner says that information quality is not just an issue that affects technologists – it's everybody's problem.

CHAPTER 5: PEOPLE – WHAT DOES A DATA GOVERNANCE TEAM LOOK LIKE?

By now, you may be thinking about the resources necessary to implement data governance. The data champion cannot do it alone. The most important aspect of implementing data governance is that people power must be used to improve the processes within an organization. Technology will have its place, but it's most importantly the people who set up new processes who make the biggest impact.

It's important to remember that these are indeed roles, not necessarily job titles. If your company is small and still working on some of the first data governance projects, data governance and stewardship roles may only be a small to moderate part of the overall responsibilities. As you begin to prove your success, the roles can be expanded into full-time roles.

Data governance roles and responsibilities

In my experience in dealing with companies that are starting a data governance program, there are key roles to get the program jumpstarted.

Executive sponsor – A c-level executive as executive sponsor is important to success. The decision on which key corporate officer to use may come down to who is available and what type of data is the biggest source of grief for the organization. Chief finance officers may be involved, especially in financial services companies, if data holes are causing risk and compliance issues. CFOs may be more apt to help you with the metrics and crunch the numbers around

ROI. Chief marketing officers will be the sponsor if problems with customer data are the issue, because they want to market properly. CIOs and CEOs may also take the role in a data governance team.

On a daily basis, the executive sponsor can provide substantial value to the data governance team. For example, if the corporation is trying to pull back on funding, the executive sponsor can communicate with the Board and management on the importance of the data governance initiative. The sponsor helps the data governance team get the resources they need to be a success.

The executive sponsor may also be somewhat of a cheerleader, heralding the benefits of information quality to the boardroom. The data champion should prepare the executive sponsor to be ready at any time with an elevator pitch fine-tuned for the board. If you recall, I mentioned that the elevator pitch is the 15-second version of the goals and benefits of the data governance team. For the board, they want to hear things like the improvement in governance, risk and compliance (GRC) that the initiative will bring. They'll want to know about the impact of data on corporate value.

Bear in mind that if you are just starting your data governance initiative with a single project, the executive sponsor may have only mild interest. You haven't proven the value of data governance yet and therefore you may not have their complete attention. That's why it's most important on the first project to take baseline measurements of information quality and track improvements. We'll cover that that subject in depth in the next chapter.

Project manager – The project manager, commonly also the data champion, plays a critical role in handling all communication, coordination, change management, and escalations come through this individual or team. The project manager usually has a bit of technical background, even temper, can build relationships, and great organizational and communication skills. After all, this person must be trusted by both the business and technologists on the data governance team.

Every day, the project manager should use their management skills to keep the team interested and engaged. The project manager should be schooled in the best methodologies for deployment, as well as the best practices and methodologies to achieve success. The project manager should always be aware of risks to project success and look for ways to mitigate risk. Finally, the project manager should be a good wing-man for the executive sponsor by being able to answer any concerns that require a more in-depth knowledge of the project.

Business stakeholder – Key business stakeholders are important to the project in their comprehension of the data. They provide the context of the data, knowing where the data is coming from and where it needs to go. These are the subject matter experts who understand what is needed from the data in order to achieve success. This person should have an intimate knowledge of the business processes used in the organization, especially in the business area in which the data will be used.

Day to day, this business user offers insight into how the data will be used. They will participate in the data profiling process, since they know how the data is used. As the governance project progresses, this team member will be involved with defining the business rules. They will be involved in all phases of the project, not just the analysis and business rule definition.

Data stewards – Your data stewards are your technologists on your team, supporting systems and access to data. They work on the more technical aspects of the project, like designing the metadata mappings and working with the tools. The data stewards will have a good working knowledge of the low-level anomalies in your data. They will know what the information it contains and the information it doesn't.

Capable data stewards must be challenged to rise above the technical jargon and communicate with business on some level. They will work with the project managers to translate the business policies and definitions created by the business stakeholders into technical requirements that can be implemented by technologists.

Every day, a data steward would be involved in activities like creating data profiling reports, aggregating the reports so that the different audiences can see the benefit of data governance. On the other hand, they will be involved managing the data model, setting up workflows, accessing the data and handling other technical requirements.

Data governance council

Many companies use the roles we've outlined to eventually form a data governance council. The existence of the council follows past successes of data governance, when data governance is proven and the corporation allocates more resources to it. There is no set number of people who should be on the data governance council. The number of each of these council members depends on the size of the company, the company's commitment to data governance and the size of the project.

A data governance council creates a de facto standard of better data management in an organization. If you want to grow data governance beyond the bounds of one or two projects, some companies structure a data governance center of excellence, a formal, permanent organization with a charter.

A data governance council might be started and managed by a steering committee made up of senior managers from the various business units who have a stake in improving data management. Similar to the roles and responsibilities played in a single data governance project, the data governance council consists of:

- chair – data champion
- executive sponsor
- business stakeholders
- data stewards.

There may be others involved in the data governance council, too. The managers of the business stakeholder and data stewards might be called in to help support the team or manage the human resource portion of the task.

Third-party advisory

If data governance is new to the organization, it is extremely helpful to bring in a third-party advisor to help steer the ship. Why? A third-party expert with experience in helping solve data problems will have a stronger voice than a data steward in the back office of the company. An impartial voice, solely focused on improving efficiency with data governance can be a catalyst for forming cohesion about the issue.

The good news is that there are many options for bringing in some outside help. Today, the major consulting firms all have data governance practices. There are smaller, more focused, boutique consulting firms that perhaps are more likely to station you with consultants who have really done data governance work. Finally, you can use the consulting arm of your well-known enterprise application vendor to be that independent voice you need to proclaim the importance of data governance.

By bringing in an independent voice, you will reinforce the purpose, value, decisions and strategies of the data governance team to the organization, and that's important for getting momentum. The third parties also bring ready access to industry information – what's working, what's not – and the experience of having done data governance in the past. Finally, a consultant will let you know how well the company is doing against other companies in your industry, and that will help you stay competitive.

Team performance goals

Despite all the virtues of data governance, don't expect participation to be enthusiastically met when it comes to the long-term goals of your data governance teams. You must work with the managers of your data stewards and business users to set priorities and reward them when they do the work.

It is often helpful to put objectives in place for team members. The objectives should be clear, measurable, and define a timetable. The following are some sample work objectives:

- Identify data-quality anomalies in the XYZ data set and reduce the number of anomalies to less than 2% by 15 January 2010. The data anomalies will be defined as those anomalies outside the data definitions. The data definitions will be defined by the data governance team by 4 April 2009.
- Design, develop and implement a system preventing erroneous and mistyped name and address data from entering the customer relationship system. This system is to be operational by 15 January 2009 and, by 15 February 2009, should contain one month's data. By 1 July 2009, the system should be capable of cleansing and repairing names and addresses from North America and the UK. By 1 October 2009 the system should also support addresses from Australia and Germany.
- By the end of the first reporting period, and by the end of each reporting period thereafter, identify at least two work process improvements having quantifiable operational or financial benefits.
- Within the next six months, reduce the penalties associated with shipping to incomplete or incorrect addresses to under 2% of all shipments.

As you can see from the last example, work objectives can be short and sweet. As you can see from the first two, that is not always the case.

Methodologies

It's at this point I should talk about data quality and data governance methodologies that influence your data governance initiative. Companies may use different methodologies to help manage the data governance program. Reading more about these can help you design your own program. I will mention a few of the more popular places to seek more specific information about methodologies, as follows:

- *Ten Steps to Quality Data and Trusted Information* is a book written by Danette McGilvray, an experienced data quality consultant who essentially details a comprehensive data quality framework. This book and accompanying website have a lot of practical templates and processes you can replicate in your project.
- The DGI Data Governance Framework offered by the Data Governance Institute is a logical structure for organizing your data governance program. Gwen Thomas is founder and president of the Data Governance Institute and has spent time in the trenches managing information quality in some very large companies. Certainly some of the methodologies developed here could help you in your own program.
- Six Sigma is a business management strategy, originally developed by Motorola, which can be used for many management processes, including data governance. Six Sigma's use is often extended to other types of business processes. It uses statistical methods to track "defects" and specific processes to reduce them. In Six Sigma, a defect is defined as anything that could lead to customer dissatisfaction.
  If you're a Six Sigma shop, you can apply some of these methods to data governance. Those who use Six Sigma as a data governance methodology tell me that it may have to be modified. Six Sigma was originally designed

for tracking and limited manufacturing defects, while tracking data defects is not so cut and dry.
- MIT has a Total Data Quality Management program which produces a large number of publications and hosts an international conference in this field. I have participated in that conference for several years now, and find it to be very valuable. The MIT IQ program publishes papers and studies on information quality. They have also designed courses of study and certificate programs at various universities across North America.

No matter what methodologics you use, you still have to roll them up into business metrics for them to be digested by the corporation, and that's really the topic of the chapter that follows.

CHAPTER 6: PAINTING THE PICTURE

Now that you've worked your way through the approval process and you've designated a team, it's time to get to work planning and delivering projects. The planning process is made of a series of meetings that set the scope, the expectations of the team and highlight the challenges they will face in making the data fit for business use.

The results of the meetings are usually integrated into a written document that can be viewed and edited by the team. Luckily, there are a number of modern-day communication vehicles available today to manage the team and communicate the plan.

Mission statement

Every organization, including your data governance team, has a purpose or a mission. Some organizations find it useful to communicate both the mission and goals of a data governance initiative. The distinction between mission and goals is that the mission is the paragraph that describes high-level objectives of the team, while goals are the specific steps to articulate the process.

The mission statement should discuss the needs and opportunities that exist, what the data governance team is doing to meet those needs and a set of values for the team. The mission statement should tally with the mission statement of the organization with regard to values. The mission statement should both define why the data governance organization exists and set a clear, definable goal for the future. The goals should then define the specific steps to reach the objective of the mission.

The data governance mission statement could revolve around any of the following key components:

- increasing revenue
- lowering costs
- reducing risks (compliance)
- avoiding data disasters
- competing effectively in the market
- meeting the organization's objectives.

Most importantly, a mission statement and the specific team goals should be inspiring to the team and to management. Be passionate and inspirational and use that passion to inspire your company with a vision of all that is possible from your data governance program.

Communication strategies

If data governance is about enabling people to improve processes, your team should work on strategies to communicate. The company needs to know things like the progress of the project, the return on investment, problems and challenges to overcome and more.

Remember though, your data governance team may be made up of executives, business people and technologists. It doesn't make sense to communicate the same information to the data stewards of a data governance team as you would to the executives on the team.

Many companies find it useful to address three audiences with their communication strategy:

- **Company** – Communicate the highlights of the data governance program, benefits, and the need for everyone to participate in managing data.
- **Data governance team** – Communicate timelines, issues with data access, data context issues, reports from data profiling, successes at a project level, project team goals and status.
- **Stewardship** – Communicate specific details of data extracts, data models, metadata management, technologies used, technical challenges.

Recognizing this separation of audiences and speaking to them in different ways is a great way to prevent the masses from being overloaded with technical jargon, but provides enough meat for your entire data governance team to be effective.

Having productive meetings

When you're trying to align a cross-functional team on your data governance initiative, it's important to have productive meetings. It's all about respect and making good use of everyone's time. The quality of your meetings will be a factor in how well you generate momentum for the data governance project. Ineffective meetings will cause the project to fizzle, while effective meetings will keep the project moving forward. Some tips for effective meetings include the following:

- Make sure you have a purpose for the meeting. Hold meetings to make decisions that can't be made by a single team member.

- Invite key decision makers and, even if they don't show up, make the decision anyway. If some of your data governance team members have scheduling challenges, let them assign proxies to make decisions on their behalf.
- Be ready for the meeting by providing attendees with information ahead of time. This will give your team the opportunity to look over any pertinent information and afford them time to think about it.
- Have a set agenda and set of objectives, and don't stray from them. We all want to hear what you did this weekend, but not in our data governance meeting.
- Start and end on time. Start on time and do not take time out of the meeting to help late arrivals catch up.
- Establish rules of meetings and make sure everyone follows them. Make sure that the data governance team knows that if you don't show up for a meeting, the decisions may be made without them.

Finally, make sure you accommodate for both the glib and those who prefer to mull over decisions on your team. All too often, those who are the first to articulate win because you'll think if it sounds smart, it probably is. The problem is, there are people in your meeting who are more pragmatic and those who like to think over important decisions. How often have you been in a meeting listening to the more persuasive members of your team, while other smart folks are sitting back? It's only when you ask them specifically to give their opinion that a brilliant idea comes out, often cutting the glib to the quick. Provide the more pragmatic members of your team with a voice by asking them outright.

Tools to communicate

Tools that supplement your in-person meetings can track progress, promote the power of data governance, help you take on difficult challenges and keep a record of successes. The good news is that there are some fantastic software tools, as well as new Web 2.0 tools that can support communications.

Workflow

Workflow software are powerful collaboration tools and should be considered to improve efficiency into your data governance process. With workflow tools, teams can manage the processes and coordination of the data governance team. The processes managed with workflow tools might include any of the following:

- work progress of a person or group
- business approval processes
- challenges of specific data governance technical processes, like ETL, data profiling or application integration
- financial approval processes.

Much of the work involved in data governance is discussing status. Workflow software can save the time and human capital investment that goes into holding status meetings by covering status and progress in an application. Employees update their status on a specific task, while managers can see what is on schedule and what is behind.

Particularly if your data governance team is global, you can improve efficiency with workflow software. If teams are in different time zones, it will be difficult for you to hold status meetings at a time that's convenient for all. A team using workflow software would post their status in the tool and decrease the number of meetings necessary for management.

Some examples of workflow tools include AtTask™, Basecamp®, Clarizen, OnStage, Microsoft Sharepoint®.

Wikis

The online encyclopedia Wikipedia is perhaps one of the best-known wikis, but you can set up your own wiki for your data governance project. A wiki is a page or collection of web pages designed for users to contribute or modify content. In your data governance projects, you can use a wiki to document processes and have an open online dialogue about risks and challenges. Wikis can hold the latest corporate data policies. Wikis can be opened up to the corporation and provide communications across the enterprise.

There are a lot of wikis to choose from. Your best bet is to check out the matrix at *www.wikimatrix.org.*

Blogs

A blog (short for "web log") is a website written by an individual with regular entries of commentary, descriptions of events, or other material, such as graphics or video. Blogs are a great ways to put a face on your data governance initiative. A well-liked team member can provide commentary or news on your data governance project. The writer may use text, images and links to other blogs written by other team members to inform and foster teamwork.

A blog allows for one person's perspective on the data governance project, but readers can leave comments and links to their own blogs. Blogs can educate and inform data governance groups, and they can use them to debate unresolved issues or to continue discussions between meetings. For educational purposes, for example, a blog could provide information about why one project was chosen over another. Blogs could also provide updates on projects and actively request reader feedback.

Data governance teams could designate certain team members to blog each week about the problems they are trying to solve and the projects they are working on. As the writer becomes better known for their blog antics, the project will become better known and accepted. Over time, this type of blog would help keep a record of the processes used – what works and what doesn't. It can also be used to inform data stewards, data governance teams and other readers about how the company is working to solve data quality issues.

RSS feeds

The problem with blogs is that you have to revisit them frequently in order to keep up on the latest news. RSS feeds are a great way to push information from the blogs to people. RSS describes a news data format used to publish frequently updated works – such as blog entries. Google and Yahoo offer gadgets that you can add to your home page, or any feed reader, to receive timely updates on the project. Whether it is updates to a project task or a podcast highlighting a unique data quality issue, RSS feeds help streamline and improve the efficiency of information distribution. Using an RSS feed to push crucial data governance information to the team benefits them by improving communication.

Getting the data

Communication aside, you really cannot underestimate the challenges in getting access to important data for your project. In large organizations, just being aware of what data exists and how to get access to it can represent a huge challenge to the success of the project. While developing a plan, you first must consider both data awareness and data access:

- **Data awareness** – What data exists in the company that could assist us in our project? Where did the data come from, and what it is used for today? Based on this, is our confidence in this data high enough for our project?
- **Data access and acquisition** – Can we access the data in a reasonable amount of time? Who controls the data? Is there an optimal window for accessing the data when it is not in use? Can the architecture handle the extra loading and unloading of data?

Getting access to the data is easily something you can underestimate. Running a data extract may seem like an easy task, but the data owners are usually busy fighting fires. The systems people may be busy working on other tasks. Team members may be on leave or otherwise out of the office. Make sure you allot enough time and give big lead times to those who will give you data access.

Data governance workshops

The planning of a data governance initiative should begin with a data governance workshop. This is a meeting or series of meetings to highlight the impact of data governance on the entire organization. When you announce the workshop, the stated goals should be to identify the linkage between data issues and business processes.

But behind the scenes, the meeting should point out gaps in the current process and solicit suggestions for process improvements to fix them. Be careful to sell the promise of data governance to the organization, while going easy on fear, uncertainty and doubt at this stage. Chances are that some of the people in the room are in charge of the faulty processes.

The workshop begins to set expectations and the scope of the data governance initiative. Of course, more detail will be necessary to flesh out these expectations, but the meeting should begin to build pragmatic, actionable steps for delivering business benefits to the organization.

To pull off a data governance workshop, you will have to have some access to the data and develop a data quality scorecard; and this requires access to data profiling and data discovery tools.

These meetings are often most successful when led by good communicators who can promote the value of data governance to the organization. If you don't feel you have someone who can run a data governance workshop, turn to your top tier consultant, or even your tools vendors for support. Most vendors who have a value to offer in the data governance space will be willing to share their experiences from other companies they've worked with.

For each decision made, thought should be given to recycling the processes. The team should always leverage what they've done on previous projects to shorten implementation time and costs on the next.

Building a useful data quality scorecard

In order to know if you're winning in the fight against poor data quality, you have to keep score. Please go back and read that sentence again, because it's probably the most important one in the book. Your team has to keep score in order to maintain long-term success with data governance.

It's surprising how many data governance teams don't do this and suffer the consequences. It may be that right now the company is behind your data governance initiative wholeheartedly. With such support, why spend the extra time tracking the benefits of data governance? The short answer is that things change. Bosses retire. Companies acquire other companies or merge, building new teams and new leadership. Companies reorganize, sometimes frequently. It would be a shame if you had to justify your team's value to new leadership without having the numbers to back it up. You have to keep score.

Practitioners use data quality scorecards to understand the detail about quality of data in a database and aggregate those scores into business value metrics. The technical metrics combined with the business metrics allow business users and technical users to collaborate on the issues with data quality.

If done right, a data quality scorecard can give the team an in-depth understanding of the task at hand. Technologists will understand the data available and the transformations that need to take place. Business users will recognize the technical challenges with the data, but also get a good idea about what data is available and how it could help them grow the business.

It's important to aggregate the information you get from a data profiling tool into business metrics. A simple non-aggregate score is usually rather meaningless. If we show that 7% of all fields are nulls, for example, the number is of no use – there is no context. You can't say whether it is good or bad, and you can't make any decisions based on this information. There is no value associated with the score.

Most data profiling tools and scorecards give you very technical metrics by default. More and more data profiling tools being developed today allow you to aggregate the technical scores into business metrics, but since a tool can't natively and unthinkingly know your business, it's up to you and the business stakeholders in the room to give it meaning.

Views of data quality scorecard

Your plan must be to make data quality scorecards for different internal audiences – marketing, IT, c-level and so on. You must design the scorecards to meet the needs of the interest of the different audiences. The initial output of a data profiling tool is information about data quality of individual data records. This is the default report that most profilers will deliver. Your job must be to aggregate scores from technological statistics into higher-level business metrics that are more meaningful and more descriptive of the value of information quality. Along the way, you will find useful metrics, allowing your team to analyze and summarize data quality from different perspectives. If you define the objective of a data quality assessment project as calculating these different aggregations, you will have a much easier time maturing your data governance program. The business users and c-level will begin to pay attention.

Which key metrics do I track?

The question of metric selection is important to a winning data governance strategy. However, the metrics have to fold up into business metrics. The aggregation might look something like this:

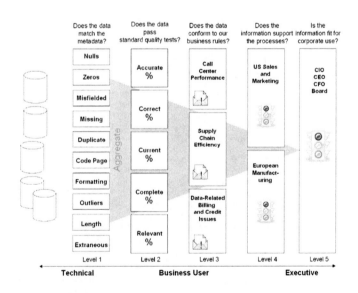

Figure 8: Aggregation of information quality metrics

The diagram describes the aggregation of information quality metrics, starting on the left with the technical aspects of data.

Level 1 – Raw data quality metrics

As technologists profile your data sets, they begin to see missing data, zeros when there should be values, misfielded data, duplicates and near duplicates, and so on. At this level, the metrics show how data anomalies are affecting your metadata management and messing up your schemas. At this level, you can't understand exactly how these data anomalies affect the business, but they begin to show that something is wrong.

As an aside, these types of data checks have existed for a long time – since the beginning of the relational database. Dr Edgar Codd, who worked for IBM in the 1960s and 70s, devised the original concept of a relational database. Dr Codd's ideas about relational databases, storing data in cross-referenced tables, were largely ignored at IBM. It was only when Larry Ellison grabbed onto the idea, and began to have success with a little company named Oracle, that IBM did finally pay attention. Today, relational databases are everywhere, including no doubt, in your company in the projects you're working on.

Even then, Dr Codd advised about data integrity. He wrote about:

- **Entity integrity** – every table must have a primary key and the column or columns chosen to be the primary key should be unique and not null.

- **Referential integrity** – consistency between coupled tables. With certain values, there are obvious relationship between tables. The same ZIP code should always refer to the same town, for example.
- **Domain integrity** – defining the possible values of a value stored in a database, including data type and length. So, if the domain is a telephone number, the value shouldn't be an address.

He put everything else into something he called "business rules" to define specific standards for your company. An example of a business rule would be for companies that store vehicle identification numbers (VINs) for data on autos – there may be a check to make sure the VIN matches the stored manufacturer, model and manufacture date. The VIN field would have a certain length and data shape – domain integrity – but also have certain character combinations to designate make and model – business rules.

The point is, information quality is not something new. It was something that the database pioneers even knew theoretically in the 1970s. Yet many companies are just learning its importance. Database applications of today and those of the past have always allowed us to break the rules, and we've done so. Sometimes it is easier to break the rules as a quick fix rather than following them to the letter. There is also a certain amount of ignorance at fault, too. Unless you've memorized the edicts of Dr Codd, your database programmers may have not even paid heed to referential integrity, and this has led to our need for data governance.

Level 2 – Business importance

In an effort to improve processes, the database technicians should roll up the data into metrics into slightly higher formulations. In their book *Journey to Data Quality*, authors Lee, Pipino, Funk and Wang correctly suggest that making the measurements quantifiable and traceable provide the next level of transparency to the business. The metrics may be rolled up into a completeness rating; for example, if your database contains 100,000 postal codes and 3,500 records are incomplete, 3.5% of your postal codes failed and 96.5% pass. Similar simple formulas exist for accuracy and correctness. Currency and relevance require a little more knowledge of how the data is being used, but not much.

Actually, Dr Wang's (et al.) theories are a brilliant extension of Dr Codd's original work about integrity. As we began to use the relational database more and more, the need for evolving the scores into something more relevant for business became more apparent.

So, if you're looking at initial results from a data profiling tool and the business users are asking you "How complete are my postal code tables?" you have the perfect answer. Unfortunately, they won't ask you that. This first aggregation still doesn't support data governance, because business users aren't thinking that way.

This level of aggregation also considers the business to a small extent. Let's face it, you're going to have a lot of tables to examine. The tables you examine, however, should be tied to the business processes your team wants to address. For example, is it important for the business to know that a customer may have participated in a promotional program in 1990, or is it more important to have current contact information for the customer? The answer depends upon the goals of the business, and your data governance team has to account for that.

Similar results don't always have the same business meaning. For example, let's say you were looking at a date field in a customer database. Without knowing too much about it, it would seem like having nulls in the date field would be a very, very bad thing. The data is incomplete and the completeness score should reflect it. However, let's say that the date field in this case just so happened to contain account cancellation date information. The null simply means that the customer associated with it has not cancelled. Now the completeness score of the data takes on new meaning. Having the data incomplete is a good thing.

That's why the mantra of data governance is that technologists and business users must work together to define what good data is. Data interpretation and configuration of the data rules cannot reside with the technologists alone. It's also why data profiling must be aggregated to the next business level.

This level of aggregation is a view back into our data when we need it and a stepping stone to a higher view. As you get into the higher levels of aggregation, you will be required by the business to understand why certain values are corrupt; you'll need this level of detail to backtrack into the data to understand the source of corruption without having to look through countless profiling reports.

Level 3 – Project importance

The next level of data quality score aggregation incorporates even more business impact. Simply put, business has processes that are supported, and the data must meet those requirements.

Example 1 – Customer relationship management system

A company wants to ensure that proper contact information is being gathered by the call centers. The business requires name, address, telephone number and e-mail address. They also want to know the customer's preferred method of contact for direct mail compliancy laws. In turn, the company will use this information to sell more products to increase revenue and bill by e-mail to lower costs.

A score can be developed based on the following criteria:

- Is the name complete?
- Is there a complete and accurate address?
- Is there a complete and accurate telephone number?
- Is there a complete and accurate e-mail?
- Has the customer specified the preferred contact method and is that data one of five specific values?
- Is the customer on the state or federal "DO NOT CALL" list? These are government-run programs that allow people to opt out of junk mail.
- How many of the names are duplicates or near duplicates?
- Does my address verification software comprehend the address?

Now, likely, there would be much more to it. For example, your company might want a way to figure out whether the person in your database is physically dead or alive. Relatives of the dead may inform you of this unfortunate circumstance, or you can get enrichment data from data providers and occasionally check data against public records. Likewise, these service providers can provide verification that a contact hasn't moved or even been sent to prison. All of those facts and many more would likely be important to the CRM system and the marketing project. The team must collaborate and determine the most important metrics.

But for simplicity's sake, let's stick with our metrics. The scores can be weighted, assigning each of the questions a level of importance. An example of a weighting might look something like this:

Score	Test	Business value
Name	The name is not blank, contains two or more characters in the name fields	Medium. This program calls for use of "Resident" in place of name. % in compliance times weight 10
Address	Is the address understood by the data quality tool	High. Several direct mail pieces are planned. % in compliance times weight 20
e-mail	Does the data follow the xxxx@yyyy.zzz (or other standard e-mail address) format? Is the field null? Does the field contain common bogus values like	Low. Although eventually important, the plan for this project is to use direct mail. % in compliance times weight 5

	"a@a.com'	
Contact Preference	Does the contact preference contain one of the five pick-list values?	Medium. Customer satisfaction impact. % in compliance times weight 10
Do Not Call	The name and address does not match (or fuzzy match) the government DO NOT CALL list.	High. Significant fines can be levied if not in compliance. % in compliance times weight 20
Duplicate	The address is not an exact match or close match to other addresses in the database?	High. Postage savings. Customer satisfaction issues caused by double mailings. Effort of company to stay green. % in compliance times weight 20
Total score		SUM of the scores/SUM of the weights (85) = Confidence in using the list.

If we were to run 100,000 records through our data profiling solutions, the results might look something like this:

Score	Test results	Weighted score
Name	81,324 of 100,000 records complied	.813 * 10 = 8.13
Address	77,201 of 100,000 records complied	.772 * 20 = 15.44
e-mail	23,129 of 100,000 records complied	.231 * 5 = 1.155
Contact Preference	99,099 of 100,000 records complied	.99 * 10 = 9.9

Do Not Call	99,757 of 100,000 records complied	.997 * 20 = 19.94
Duplicate	85,002 of 100,000 records complied	.85 * 20 = 17
Total score		71.565 / 85 = 84% confidence in this data source

Now the individual results can be tracked over time to understand the data governance team's impact on the suitability of the data.

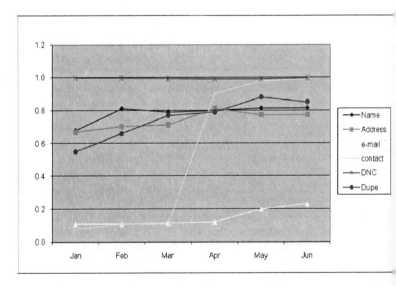

Figure 9: Data quality tracking

A few observations about this level of aggregation:

- You can see the impact of our data cleansing activities in March. You discovered a comments field that contained contact preference information in the database.
- You can begin to see that the call center training in May is having a positive impact on gathering e-mail.
- We're assuming that the number of names and address will change month to month, so you must track percentages.
- For this mailing, it is more important to ensure that those on the DO NOT CALL list are not bothered. Since we're tracking unweighted scores, you can't see the distinction between important and less important values yet.

The team can also track the weighted combined score to track the data suitability to the mission over time.

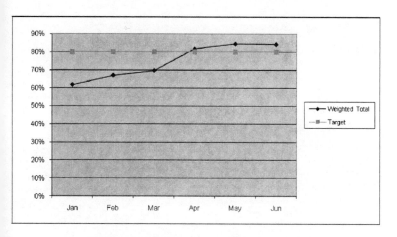

Figure 10: Weighted combined score

In this chart, the data governance team has established that a weighted score of 80% is good enough to begin marketing to the list. The suitability of the data crossed the threshold of suitability in April. As depicted by the chart, the data governance team has made huge gains in how efficiently the marketing team mails promotional pieces and the suitability of the data.

Of course, you'll want to track the amount of money saved, too. After all, ROI is the most important aspect of data governance. In this example chart, I've set the number of customers at 100,000 and the price of the mailings at $2. If the conditions of the mailing list did not comply with our tests, we can assume that the piece is wasted, either by being disregarded by the customer or not reaching its intended target. We can track that wastage over time.

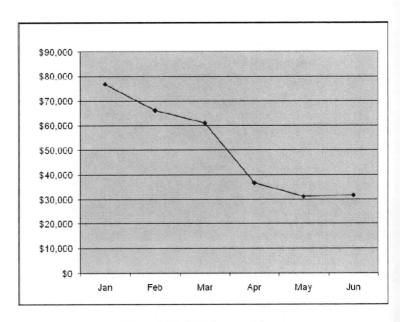

Figure 11: Mailing wastage

This chart makes for a compelling argument for the whole company to embrace data governance. In January, nearly $80,000 was being wasted each month because of poor data quality. Today, we spend nearly $50,000 less in wasted mailing costs due to our data governance initiative.

Example 2 – Supply chain

Another example of this level of scorecard would be when a company wants to ensure that their ERP and SCM (supply chain management) systems support an efficient supply chain. In doing so, they will reap rewards from their ability to carry the correct inventory levels and their ability to negotiate with their vendors. After all, their worldwide buying power is immense, even though when data exists in global data silos, it is difficult to have an overall view and know buying power correctly. The company investigates consolidating worldwide ERP and SCM systems.

In terms of carrying costs, it's well known that money and other resources (for example, space) are tied up when inventory is held. Manufacturing companies, often say (with tongue somewhat in cheek) that inventory is evil – it incurs costs carrying it. Typical figures used by professionals in supply chain vary anywhere from 15% to 40%. The costs include:

- Capital costs or opportunity cost – Tying money up in inventory prevents you from spending money on other things, like sales and marketing.
- Cost of space – You have to manage storage space for inventory and, in doing so, you have to rent or buy the space, heat it and light it.

- Handling cost – You usually have to pay staff to move items around in your warehouse. They need forklifts and carts to complete their work.
- Obsolescence – Items sitting in your warehouse will become obsolete and that costs money.
- Spoilage, pilferage and accidental damage – That acetone inventory you keep is tricky. Not only do employees take it for their home cleaning projects, but oops, it just spilled on a container of plastic parts.
- Insurance – Paying an insurance company to protect you against fire, floods, earthquakes and other "acts of God."

Inventory management professionals use something called "Economic Order Quantity" or EOQ as the magic number to understand the level of inventory that minimizes the total inventory holding costs and ordering costs. It's clear that given these costs, you don't want to hold more than you need to in inventory.

What's less known, however, is that by fixing data quality issues, you can also lower costs of holding inventory.

To illustrate this phenomenon, let's take a look at some of the basic data quality problems that can occur in a procurement system, either SCM or ERP. Let's look at how we can identify problems and how to track them. In the diagram, we show four parts that exist in the system. If there were only these four parts, we would easily be able to identify:

- Parts 1 and 2 are likely a match. If we apply standardization to both the part number and the description, the parts align perfectly. Our procurement data governance team member confirms.

- Parts 1 and 3 are obviously not a match, despite the fact that they have the same part number. We might use description and supplier to determine this, or we can rely on the data governance team member from procurement to help us.
- Parts 1 and 4 are not a match, but can be substituted, according to the description field. Our procurement team member tells us that XL-56699 is now obsolete and the supplier has a new model XM-56699 that has a lower cost and is updated with more reliable parts.

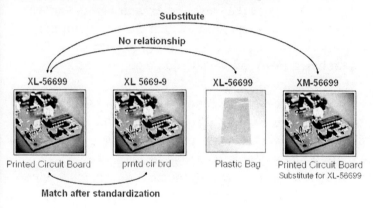

Figure 12: Relationship between parts

So, what can we learn from this? By understanding all of these relationships, we can benefit from a business perspective in a couple of ways:

- We don't need to have three Parts 1, 2 and 4 all in inventory, since they are either a match or a substitution. Good thing, too, since this circuit board costs $5000. It will free up capital for us.

- When you buy parts from a vendor, it is often the case that the vendor finds ways to lower costs with subsequent models. The XL model is priced higher than the XM model, but they do exactly the same thing. Having the ability to connect the two items as substitutions will lead to cost savings.
- As orders come in, we need to verify if an order for part number XL-56699 is a circuit board or a plastic bag. Since carrying costs are so expensive, mistakes in this area can be costly. We'll need to update that part number.
- In examining the database and all four variations, we need to let the supplier know that we are eligible for quantity discounts. With so many circuit boards purchased this year, we should be getting the lower price on the pricing sheet.

By the way, the procurement team tells you that XL-56699 plastic bags are very big bags, come by the gross and are shipped on a pallet. Does your facility have a loading dock? No? Well, the shipping company does charge us fees when the receiver can't accept shipment. We should include a field that describes the package size and handling instructions.

So, for supply chain data, the data governance team needs to track the quality of inventory data. A score can be developed based on the following criteria:

- Are the parts listed in the procurement system truly unique?
- Do the descriptions of parts follow a set format, or are duplicate parts obscured by differences in abbreviations, descriptive text order, size designation, color and so on?
- Is all the relevant information available, like form factor, quantity per box and shipping requirements?
- Are there cost-saving part substitutions?

Levels 4 – Business importance

Levels 4 and 5 are aggregations rolled up to decisions that are made by corporate management. In the case of Level 4, business users simply want to know if the data is ready to support business processes. They'll want to know if the data going into their systems supports their business processes. If not, who needs to adjust to make them ready? Often the results of Level 3 are used to aggregate traffic light indicators for Level 4. The business users can have confidence that the data is ready for business use, while the data stewards and technologists can keep an eye on the lower aggregation levels to respond to any issues that arise.

Level 4 is powerful in that it provides complete cross-functional visibility into data governance policies. Publicize it. If anyone in the company for any reason causes the indicator to go from green to yellow, or – God forbid – to red, the entire company can learn from this from the impact. The Level 4 aggregations can be used to police data governance processes in this manner. On the other hand, if the call center is consistent in providing fit-for-use customer data that meets the needs of marketing for the entire quarter, for example, positive reinforcement could be given, either in public praise or monetary bonuses.

Level 5 – Executive performance

Level 5 and aggregates up to the executive level, who generally want to know if the data is "GO" or "NO GO". Where Level 4 provides a score, Level 5 provides a traffic light approach, giving executive easy insight into the data governance program. If some event were to disrupt compliance, the executive would know immediately and be able to drop the hammer.

The number of traffic lights showing unit data integrity would grow as new data governance projects came online.

Drill-downs

The level of detail obtained through these various levels of aggregation provide a complete top-down understanding of information quality issues and give the data governance team the power to improve processes. Today, these reports can be generated by using a combination of data profiling tools and business intelligence (BI) software. The metrics generated by the profiler are fed into the BI tool to generate charts, graphs and dashboards.

However, the data profiling vendors are seeing the call for these tools and more are coming on the market. When you want to investigate data quality, the drill-downs are available to the data stewards and champions. The layers are necessary to better understand the causes, nature and magnitude of the data problems.

Scorecards, aggregations and compliance

Of course, at the very bottom of the data quality scorecard aggregation are reports showing the quality of individual records or subjects. The data itself is a very useful way to see data anomalies. However, this atomic level view should be used sparingly when security and compliance are at issue. Pharmaceutical data, health care data, financial data are examples where businesses must be extra careful in allowing atomic-level views.

CHAPTER 7: FIXING YOUR DATA

Armed with solid metrics on the status of information quality, you can now begin to fix the issues. It's important to begin to establish policies for making changes to data. The data governance team needs to create new policies for data and leverage executive approval to help enforce their recommendations.

Remember, these policies should be business focused, not technology focused. They should dictate how data is handled within systems. The team needs to decide the policies for all corporate data, while keeping in mind that data is likely to be cross-organizational. While individual projects may have unique data rules, the policies should represent the shared interest of the entire organization.

The solid metrics give you another advantage. They give you a baseline against which you can measure improvement over time. Throughout the process of fixing the data, you can use the same metrics at pre-determined intervals or milestones to measure change from baseline. By publicizing the business impact of your improvement, you'll gain notoriety and begin to sell the advantages of advanced data management.

Causes and actions

At the root of the problems with managing your data are data quality problems. Traditional data quality methods do not often attack the root cause. Applications like data warehouses, for example, simply offer a process for taking dysfunctional data and aligning it for the purposes of business intelligence. If you want to get complete control of your data, you must start at the source of the bad data. You might think of this phenomenon like you would think about a dirty lake. You can clean up the lake, but you also have to clean the streams that feed into it. You can't really solve the problem until you do both.

The root cause of data quality problems vary, but commonly fall into one of the following categories:

Cause 1: Receiving merger and acquisition data

In a previous chapter, I wrote extensively about the problems with mergers and acquisitions. To accomplish more effective mergers from a data management perspective, you must integrate disjointed applications and use incongruent data sets that exist between the two companies.

Actions

- Educate executives on the challenges of data integration without using technical jargon. Make sure they understand that the quality of data can be used to negotiate business value. If a company claims to have 300,000 customers, an audit of the data may reveal that some are duplicates or bogus, and the number of customers could easily be reduced to 150,000.
- Set up a policy that plans for the data integration needs for mergers and acquisitions.
- Use data profiling (discovery) tools as early in the merger process as possible to understand data. Data

profiling will provide a clear picture of the challenges of merging data sources.

- Use data profiling after the merger to understand all of the challenges with data integration. Use the metrics to come up with a plan.
- Use data quality tools to apply data standardization to the incoming data. Data quality tools will take the same rules you applied to your internal data and apply them to the new incoming data.

Cause 2: Data ownership and control

A big reason for poor information quality is ownership of the data. If a business unit feels they should have complete control over their data, they may be tempted to create their own set of local applications that do not adhere to data standards. On the other hand, certain crucial data sources may have no apparent ownership and become the wild west of databases – also a lawless frontier.

Actions

- Publicize the benefits of your data governance program. Stress importance of data governance to business users. Market the benefit of cross-functional, enterprise-wide data management.
- Emphasize the expense of rogue IT projects and work with your CTO to ban them by showing real world examples of rogue databases and the impact of their lawlessness on the bottom line. For example, if marketing had cleansed the data before mailing, it would have saved $50,000 in postage fees.

- Leverage executive sponsorship for the data governance team to take or establish co-ownership of the data.

Cause 3: Deliberately poor or apathetic data entry

Even well-trained data-entry staff can be inconsistent or make mistakes when entering data. It can be difficult to keep a team of call center agents enthusiastic about getting every detail absolutely correct. However, the error potential increases exponentially when customers are asked to input their own information via web forms, either because of apathy, or because they are deliberately trying to obscure their identity.

Actions

- Input controls – Make extensive use of field validations, including table lookups, formulas and data-type restrictions to help remedy the problem, but be careful. Having too many restrictions will cause those who enter data to look for ways to get past the restrictions, leading to choosing an option even though it's not the correct one.
- Address correction and verification – Cleaning and validating customer data in real-time during the entry process is effective in ensuring that erroneous data does not infect your systems. Solutions can verify city, state and zip code data, as well as any type of customer-specific data. Systems will verify, correct, and properly format the addresses entered in accordance with local postal standards.

- Business rules – Applying the same business rules to other types of data will ensure that the formats and shapes of data will remain standardized.
- Profiling and dashboards – Data profiling and dashboard applications provide ways for data governance teams to track poor information coming into the systems and report back to the data source about any anomalies that have been keyed in. The profiling tool generates in-depth metrics and the dashboards provide a presentation layer.
- Incentives – The data governance team should consider a program to provide incentives to those call center employees who have the most complete information. The data governance team can track this compliance with data quality rules with data profiling tools.

Cause 4: Metadata standards

This term concerns the lack of standard methods to describe exactly what should be in any given field; there is no common data dictionary. For example, a metadata schema would specify that FNAME always contains a first name, not blanks, nor an incomplete name, nor multiple first names, nor any other types of data.

When data lacks a metadata standard, it will tend to work in a silo, where the application has been customized to handle non-conforming values. The data will do its damage when the data is migrated to a new system, however. Data governance teams must design and enforce schemas to ensure that data can be used across the business unit and eventually across the company.

Actions

- Metadata management tools – The data governance team should work to build a single definition of metadata. Sometimes this is accomplished within business units first, and then expanded enterprise-wide. Teams leverage ETL solutions for data warehouse. Leverage master data management (MDM) and application vendors for metadata models available based on industry and application.
- System upgrades – Metadata standards are best applied during an upgrade or migration of a legacy system. Chances are, there will be business drivers to upgrade your systems from time to time. Use this time to upgrade the data, too, in support of a standardized metadata model and standardized data.
- Data profiling and monitoring – Check adherence of data to the metadata definitions before moving data. Continue to check adherence to the model on a regular basis.

Cause 5: Incomplete or missing information

You may find yourself in a position where the data just doesn't exist to accomplish a business objective. For example, let's say you need to set up sales territories equally among hundreds of sales representatives working for your company. The project calls for longitude and latitude information for each contact in the prospect database. If available, this data would let the team pinpoint sales territories so that there is no mistake about sales-lead ownership. In a business-to-business market, the sales force may want Dunn & Bradstreet or Harte-Hanks demographic information available as well, in order to understand the size of the company, corporate officers and other important sales information.

Actions

- Data profiling – Having a complete understanding of what's there and what's not will give your team a more complete understanding of the challenges ahead.
- Data standardization – The data governance team should apply standards to the data with a data quality tool. This enables the third-party data sources to match up more precisely.
- Enrichment – The team should either engage a service company to append the data with the correct information or apply it in-house. Regardless, a process needs to be planned around appending the data.
- Data monitoring – The team should be careful about appending third-party data and set up a process to check the validity of third-party sources before updating. The impact of erroneous third-party data could be hard-felt. For example, if credit score data from a third-party source is erroneous, the result could be additional credit issued to unworthy customers or good, credit-worthy customers being denied credit. The team should consider the impact of any erroneous third-party data, and plan checks and balances.

These are just some of the causes of poor information quality in your organization and the actions that data governance teams should take to manage data.

Information quality and data-intensive projects

Over time, data governance begins to get baked into project plans. Whenever data-intensive applications are developed, upgraded or migrated, an effective data management process should be part of the equation.

Remember, in data governance, we constantly leverage both business users, who know the value of the data, and technologists, who can apply what the business users know to the data. Data governance teams should consider how they fit into each and every part of their project. Let's take a look at the steps of a typical project and how the data governance team fits in.

Six phases of a data-intensive project

Projects that involve large amounts of data, such as CRM, MDM, ERP, business intelligence and data warehouse projects, migrations, consolidations and upgrades, all offer the opportunity to improve data quality and therefore are great opportunities for your data governance team to become involved. When you roll out a project, the project manager plans a series of project phases that define the progress of the project. Most methodologies call for a project to have six phases, but you may have slightly more or less. The point is that each phase requires that people work together toward a certain goal. The phases are:

1 Project preparation – gathering requirements, defining a team and understanding business objectives.
2 Blueprint – writing the plan.
3 Implement – executing the action plan.
4 Rollout preparation – getting the company ready for the new project.

5 Go live – transitional period to turn on the new solution and debug new processes and technologies.
6 Maintain – tuning the processes and technologies and taking what you've learned to the next project.

Let's examine each of these project phases and how your data governance team can make an impact.

Phase 1: Project preparation

Project preparation	Blueprint	Implement	Rollout preparation	Go live	Maintain

In this phase, the project manager will evaluate what resources and time are needed to execute the project and what issues, roadblocks and risks will need to be overcome. Leverage your data governance team to help define the scope, set expectations and enumerate deliverables of the project. The data governance team is integral in conducting an analysis of the current state of your data.

Define project team and roles

During Phase 1, you must involve subject matter experts from business areas to achieve success. It's a good thing that your governance team is made up of business users and technologists. It's a good idea to have both technologists and business people because of the concepts of "syntax" and "context."

- Syntax – Technologists are capable of making data conform to a proper syntax with relative ease. An example of this might be that telephone numbers should all appear in the same format in a database.
- Context – Business stakeholders are the best source of information regarding context, or the meaning behind

the data. They'll understand if a field containing predominantly nine-digit numbers is a tax ID number, for example.

Identify business objectives

During project planning, you would assign business objectives. As part of this task, both short- and long-term data-quality goals should be identified. Short-term objectives usually relate directly to the project and activities related to data movement and manipulation. Longer-term goals usually take into consideration how the work being done on the immediate project can be leveraged by the organization and extended for further value.

In the short term, begin improving data by starting small and keeping the scope well defined. In the long term, keep in mind that if all goes well, you will have success, and you will be asked to replicate this success across the company.

Scope

Scoping draws clear parameters around the data you are capturing, moving, cleansing, standardizing, linking and enriching, and its use. Each requirement must be assessed to determine whether or not the data involved in this project can or will meet the requirement to the satisfaction of the business. There are several basic questions to answer:

1 Does the suggested data exist within the organization?
2 What source or sources contain this data?
3 What is the level of quality within each source, for this information?

4 What cleansing, standardization or de-duplication is necessary to meet the requirement?
5 What problems or anomalies must be addressed as part of this project?

In a data migration, for example, you might be looking for certain key elements to appear in the target data model. You may first need to confirm that the anticipated target data physically exists within source systems and may next need to determine the best source for the data, or the most trusted source. If taking data from multiple sources, you may have to establish a set of standards that all source systems conform to in order to produce a consistent representation of that data in the new target system.

Understanding the scope of the project early is important to its successful and timely delivery. Be sure to categorize the need-to-have data and the nice-to-have data. Be prepared to drop off the nice-to-haves if time becomes short, or if the effort of moving, cleansing, standardizing and so on outweighs the anticipated business benefit.

There are ways to limit scope. For example, if you're integrating multiple data sources, will it be one large movement of data or several smaller movements? Will the data need to be the entire database, or is six months enough? Working through these issues with the data governance team will keep the project on-time and on-target, and will help manage expectations during the project lifecycle so there are no surprises as the project nears a close.

Analyze current technology

Early in the process, it is a good idea to take inventory of the current processes for data governance that are in place. Perform interviews of the key technologists and determine what is working and what is not meeting user expectations.

If a process or technology exists that meets user expectations, can it be leveraged within the new solution? If so, can it also be leveraged for other solutions in accordance with long-term business objectives? If not, is it a good source of standards or logic, which can be designed into a new data-quality solution that offers more options for future growth?

Often solutions to data-quality problems might be point solutions, without regard to the entire enterprise. The key is to develop a solution that can serve the needs of the entire organization.

Assess data risks

Does your source data actually support the business objectives? During a data risk assessment, it is crucial to ensure that the available data satisfactorily meets business requirements. Much of the legwork for this analysis is performed by IT through mapping-data-to-requirements exercises and performing extensive data investigation of source systems. Should questions arise, key business stakeholders should immediately be involved to ensure the project is ultimately successful in delivering what the business expects.

If data does not meet expectations, what are the root causes of these gaps and how must they be addressed before proceeding with your project? Does project scope need to be revisited, or do isolated requirements need to be classified as high risk?

Use a data profiling tool on the source data to determine if the data is viable. If the data cannot support key business requirements, the project is at a high risk of failure despite investments of time and money. Thus, before committing to development, first assess data to ensure that the project can ultimately meet user expectations.

Phase 2: Making the blueprint

Project preparation	Blueprint	Implement	Rollout preparation	Go live	Maintain

In this phase, you'll assess data issues in detail and begin to build a plan for improving data as part of your overall project. The data governance team will define or use current corporate standards for data, and take a baseline measurement of your current state of data quality. The baseline will serve two purposes: it will help to enlist executive support by showing the business impact of poor data quality; and it allows you to tangibly show the improvement in the data at named milestones after the new system or solution is in production.

Define success metrics

You should have a complete understanding of how well you are doing in managing data. Success metrics are necessary to drive future investments and recognition for the data governance team. They are almost always unique to the project at hand. We talked about specific metrics in a previous chapter and how to aggregate them into business impact.

Communication strategy

A communication strategy should also be put in place early in the process. In a previous chapter, we talked about using wikis, blogs, workflow tools and similar technology to improve communication. At this stage of the project, a marketing plan of sorts needs to be part of the planning.

Define standards

With every business, there are certain standards that can be applied to every piece of data. For example, a name and address should almost always conform to postal standards. E-mail addresses conform to a certain shape with a user name, internet domain and an "@" sign in the middle. However, there may be data for which your team needs to define a new standard. This is typically a part number, item description, supply chain data, and other non-address data. For this, you need to set the definition with the business team. As part of the process, profile the data and explore it to decide what special data exists in your required fields. Then establish system standards that can then be automated and monitored for compliance.

Access data

At this point in design, it is necessary to look into data extracts to understand what mappings, transformations, processing, cleansing and so on must be established to create and maintain data that meets the needs and standards of the new system or solution. Technologists are responsible for defining data extracts and gaining appropriate access to source systems.

The data governance team should not underestimate the time it takes to access the data. It may be difficult to track down who owns the data and if there is an optimal window for extracting it. Make sure you allot enough time and give long lead times to those who will give you data access.

Analyze source data

Employ advanced profiling and data discovery functions for comprehensive column and attribute analysis. Identify potential problems within structured data fields, such as dates, postal codes, product codes, customer codes, addresses, or any attributes that should conform to a particular format and structure. Configure custom data-quality rules, and flag any attributes that do not conform.

When you're done with the analysis, you will have a very good idea of the challenges you face in integrating data and the information necessary to develop designs that address the challenges proactively. At this time, it is also a good idea to revisit the project plan and confirm that appropriate time and resources have been allocated to deal with any data issues that have been uncovered.

Capture a baseline

Business team members have defined the data-quality metrics and business impact in a previous step. Now is the time to take a baseline measurement. As part of the source system analysis, a baseline of each source system should be captured and stored as well as how multiple systems conform to expected metrics or business rules. In some cases, it will make sense to look not only at each source system in isolation, but across systems.

Data architecture and schema/data model

As the data model is being developed, a crucial step often overlooked is confirming that the source data supports the anticipated data-model design. The best way to have confidence that this is the case is to make sure that the metadata accurately describes the values. In essence, you should not assume that the metadata and system documentation accurately describes the data itself – you should prove it with profiling tools.

This step can then easily be compared and cross-referenced to intended data-model plans by the data-modeling team. It's important not to skip this step because, if the data model is broken, you could spend weeks and weeks of manual effort trying to fix it, and this will put a big red flag on your project right from the start. It may cause you to immediately begin to miss schedules and, in the worst case, cause project cancellations.

Data architecture and platforms

There are any number of different solutions that may be built as part of your overall project. The biggest consideration for a non-custom or in-house data-quality solution is whether or not the technology you are acquiring supports process execution on all platforms of the source and target systems within your given project.

Evaluate vendor tools using your longer-term vision and ensure that you have enough flexibility for future projects. In other words, don't skimp on the lower-cost desktop solution that meets the need of the project when you can use the enterprise solution that will meet your long-term goals. The data governance team should provide your organization with the flexibility to extend the data governance to different environments and on other platforms that exist within your technical enterprise infrastructure.

Develop test case scenarios

As you examine your data, you will uncover patterns and common occurrences in the data that require resolution. For example, names may appear in your CRM sources in any one of the following formats:

```
Smith, John          John Smith

Smith/John           John and Jan Smith
```

It's up to you and your business team members to decide how to standardize each of these name formats for optimal efficiency in the target systems. Should "John and Jan Smith" be linked, but separate records in your master file or remain as a single entry?

Set up a test file or database of records that present these common data situations for quality assurance (QA) purposes during this stage of the project. You will complete a QA step before you go live. This test case scenario definition effectively begins to build a list of data-quality anomalies, which you can leverage to build and test business rules and quality processes.

Define exceptions process

In a data-quality process, an exception occurs when a piece of data cannot be interpreted by the business rules and process engine your team has defined, i.e. an address does not contain enough information to be verified with the USPS standardization business rules.

When a data-quality exception occurs, the data steward must resolve the exception and decide whether the anomaly is an unusual occurrence, or whether new rules should become part of the data-quality process. Your project should define a clear way to handle exceptions from a data management perspective, including automated distribution (of error records) where possible, areas of responsibility for correcting, and a method to report anomalies back to the source.

Phase 3: Implement

Project preparation	Blueprint	Implement	Rollout preparation	Go live	Maintain

When all the planning is done, it's time to begin to put the technology in place to improve data using automation wherever possible. Despite the technical nature of this phase, business users on the data governance team still play an important role in this phase.

Create user acceptance test plan

As team members create user acceptance test (UAT) plans, additional considerations should be incorporated that investigate and display the results of data-quality processes that have been built into the new system or solution. As a result, UAT should include not only testing of new functionality and/or reports, but should also be prepared to include data-quality test case scenarios. Test data should include both good and problematic input data, so that a wider business audience (UAT resources) is forced to confirm that the data-quality processes are producing desirable results.

Create data-quality processes

During the implementation phase, the technical team puts together the data-quality process defined and designed during the Blueprint phase. This usually includes cleansing, standardization, enrichment and matching/linking processing from one of the many off-the-shelf enterprise data-quality solutions.

QA initial results

The most important part of the project should be that business users are happy with the results. As you begin to implement new data-quality process designs, project managers should have business users run sample data through the data-quality processes to ensure results meet their expectations. Business users can compare results before and after processing with profiling tools. Coarse-tune processes using sample data, then switch over to a complete data set for formal QA.

Once results have been verified, it's time to load sample data into the target applications and begin testing it more thoroughly. By taking the extra step with the business during the QA cycle, you're much more likely to be successful the first time you load data and will avoid loading and reloading data repeatedly.

Validate rules

In Phase 1 and 2, you've both determined what you have and what you need. Rules are developed in an iterative analytic process. This requires access to knowledge about intended meaning of the data. Business users and data analysts should work together on this process, applying the same technology and process described for analyzing source data, if additional questions come up. Give business users an opportunity to set up test data scenarios and allow them to review the results after the cleansing process.

Tune business rules and standards

You may find that some of the initial data-quality process design does not meet expectations or act as expected. Involving business team members directly with the tuning process ensures that the rules exactly meet their needs and removes the risk of failed expectations late in the game.

Phase 4: Rollout preparation

Project preparation	Blueprint	Implement	Rollout preparation	Go live	Maintain

During this phase of a project plan, business users and IT must determine how and when the development environment is migrated to production. Before that, however, UAT must be completed and users must be trained on the changes they will encounter when using the new system or solution. The help desk must also be properly prepared and able to answer any questions that arise as a result of new processes for data governance.

Execute user acceptance test plan

The UAT plan should include a record of the business users' sign-off of the documented scenarios and the data quality processes that influenced the project. Some different types of UAT strategies include:

- New system test – application to be tested is entirely new (not an enhancement or system upgrade).
- Regression test – amount of change in an existing application requires a full system retest.
- Limited test – amount of change in an existing application requires only change-specific testing.

It's valuable to test inside the target application, too. Things to test include:

- All forms – A data quality process can be baked into the target application to allow for checks when the users enter data. If so, this has to be part of the UAT.
- All reports – Ensure data-quality processes have not negatively affected the results from the reports, and that they are as expected.
- Test scenarios – Test the results of the data-quality process's impact on systems and applications that interface with the ones included in your project.

User training and help desk training

Users must be made aware of new applications or processes, and the help desk should know who to call to escalate any technical issues. Effective user training is a critical factor for a successful implementation. Here, the goal is simple: give your users the skills and confidence they need to use the new solution, to facilitate end-user adoption. Make them aware of:

- any new required fields or formats as they enter data into the system;
- any new screens or pop-ups requesting validation of automated cleansing and matching of data;
- the positive impact and business benefits of new, cleaner data;
- the involvement of the data governance team in creating high-quality data.

Production system cutover plan

As the system is rolled out to end users, the operations and support team should have all the tools, processes and knowledge to support them. A plan for transitioning from the project team to the operations and support team is crucial.

The decisions you need to make include training, if/how to phase the rollout, expertise needed when the cutover occurs, whether to run multiple systems (old and new) in tandem, and if so, for how long, whether to hire additional resources (for example, consultants or contractors) to assist, and any additional security considerations.

Successfully complete initial cleanse/load

For many projects, the first step of going live involves an initial load or an initial cleanse process. Data is rarely loaded without encountering errors during the extraction, transforming and loading of data. But, by taking the time upfront to thoroughly investigate source system data, incorporate necessary processing into your designs, and perform UAT that includes anticipated problematic data conditions, you have proactively addressed the issues that cause most project teams severe headaches late in the game.

Should something unexpected occur and require attention, you already have the resources and infrastructure in place to quickly react: your data governance team is already familiar with the project, the data and any technology you have been using and can swiftly look at the data and assess the problem for a quick resolution.

Phase 5: Go live

Project preparation	Blueprint	Implement	Rollout preparation	Go live	Maintain

During this phase, your team will turn on the switch and your new data-quality processes will begin to provide immediate benefits to your organization. The fruits of your labor will begin to be realized.

Problem resolution

In the early part of this phase, it's a good idea to have in place a cross-functional problem resolution team – including business analysts or departmental resources familiar with business processes, performance engineers, data architects, field technicians and contacts from any vendors – to be available on an emergency basis to provide rapid problem resolution.

The team's remit is to intervene early after a problem is identified and to provide ways by which that problem may be alleviated and the corporation can achieve the planned-for success. Beyond the typical IT staffing of this team, your data governance program will require you to empanel business subject matter experts, those who understand what the data in the tables mean, to make decisions about the data should an issue arise.

As this phase matures, all support organizations will need a more formal set of processes and procedures in place for helping to resolve user and system-generated queries, issues or problems in a consistent manner. In some organizations, these processes are very structured; in others, they are more informal.

Here is an example of an escalation hierarchy, along with the individuals who perform these tasks, for a fairly large implementation. For this example, when a problem is identified, it is escalated as follows:

- Tier 1: Help desk technicians – provide first-line support to the user community.
- Tier 2: Information professionals – typically are more aware of the data aspect of the operation than the help desk.
- Tier 3: Data stewards – depending on the nature of the problem, information professionals can contact data stewards, who tend to have an enterprise view of a data subject area, as opposed to knowledge of data and processes within a given application only.
- Tier 4: Data champion – an issue usually reaches this level if an architectural change is required to resolve it. The data champion will have to analyze the situation and take the appropriate actions to resolve it.

The hierarchy just described is merely one example of a support and escalation hierarchy. No matter what type of support hierarchy you have, it is crucial that each group within it understands its role and responsibilities with respect to data management. Moreover, the team must be able to quickly resolve or escalate any issues that arise.

Post mortem

In post mortem, you should re-run your baseline processes and collect updated results for a quantified measurement of your impact. Gather up your metrics, your support log, your exceptions processing log and other relevant documentation. Call a meeting to:

- ensure that the project met the business objectives;
- ensure that the project met the outlined success criteria;
- list the lessons learned during the project – use them as input to improve future project delivery;
- conduct performance reviews for team members;
- publicize your achievements.

Define monitoring processes

Given that all systems and processes are assumed to be operating well, it is now time to ensure that appropriate monitoring processes are in place. Regularly scheduled data audits are a great way to ensure that data continues to meet expectations and highlights any areas of quality that have slipped or new problem areas that have become evident.

To facilitate this process, many organizations leverage the technology used for risk assessment, baseline measurements, source system analysis and design, and user acceptance testing. For example, a data profiling tool in which you have trained the data governance team can easily perform scheduled audits and ongoing monitoring.

Phase 6: Maintain

Project preparation	Blueprint	Implement	Rollout preparation	Go live	Maintain

In most religions of the world, there is a day to reflect on the good work you've done, admit your shortcomings and set a plan in place to improve. Phase 6 is that day for those who believe in data governance. It is also a time of joy, however. In this phase, the fruits of your labor will be realized and you should not be shy about telling the world what you have accomplished.

Announce successes

One of the keys to maintaining funding for your project is to internally publicize the successes you've had. In reality, a data quality initiative should be constantly re-sold at every opportunity to continue to reinforce in people's minds the value you are introducing to your organization.

Ways to communicate your success include:

- using blogs, wikis and other Web 2.0 technologies;
- e-mailing a monthly data quality update;
- sending a memo from the executive sponsor about the project. Feed the sponsor business benefit information, such as money saved on marketing mailings, improved marketing sell-through rates, improved inventory and supply chain savings, etc. It may have more weight if sent by an executive;
- identifying what the business users on your team are contributing to the project, and publishing that information;
- recognizing the customers/users of the data first and how they are benefiting from your improved data.

This is also a very good time to remind the company that data quality is everyone's problem and ways they can help solve data quality issues.

Collect new requirements for next phase

With your success in hand, it's time to begin gathering requirements for the next phase. Business users will be inspired by the new intelligence available to them and begin to ask for additional data. They may want you to expand the systems exposed to your newly developed data quality process, add additional data sources to your new system or solution, or incorporate new systems and applications if your company is in acquisition mode. If you play it right, word will get out about your successes, and your solution and/or data quality services will be in demand.

CHAPTER 8: TECHNOLOGIES THAT SUPPORT
DATA GOVERNANCE

Enter a Google search on "data governance" and you'll find many companies who say they solve the data governance problem. Data quality vendors, data profiling tools, MDM platform vendors and even some of the mega vendors like Oracle and SAP will all claim to have data governance technology that makes everything so simple.

The truth is, there is no magic technology that handles all encompassing data governance. That's because data governance is about process improvements that are specific to your industry and your company. The technology is only there to assist you with certain pieces of the data governance process, but most of the burden will fall on your shoulders, as the data champion leading a company embarking on the project.

You can think about it as if you would plan for digging a hole. If you want to dig a hole, you have to decide where it will be, who will dig it and how deep it will be. Management will want to know what value the hole digging brings to the organization. The users of the hole should be part of the decision process in those areas, so as the head of the hole-digging team, you need to bring them into the job. You have to make sure that all those affected by the digging are notified. They should be delighted about the benefits of the new hole.

Technology is often just the shovel or backhoe that speeds up the process. You have to use the right tool at the right time to improve information quality and meet the business needs of the organization. We've already talked about the communication technologies like blogs and wikis. They are like the sign out in front of the hole, telling people to be cautious and advertising the company in charge of the hole digging process.

Types of data governance technologies

To assist with data governance, you might employ many different technologies, depending on the project. Technologies fall into the following categories when it comes to data governance: preventative, diagnostic and health, infrastructure and enrichment, and communication and management.

Preventative

Preventative technology stops poor information quality from coming into your organization, and therefore limits disruption. Preventative technology is often used when it's difficult to offer training to all of the people who may be involved with data entry. If your company has large call centers, or if the feeds you're getting aren't completely in your control, you may want to seek some preventative measures with these tools.

Type-ahead technology

Type-ahead technology watches the user and helps complete the data entry in real time. Commonly used for name and address data, this technology will ensure that all addresses entering your customer database are verified against local postal databases and are input in a consistent, standard format. This process improvement verifies addresses at the front end, before they are entered into the company's database. Type-ahead technologies prevent data from being entered into a database in varying formats with an unknown degree of accuracy. The application is usually small and may sit on top of Siebel, Microsoft CRM, SAP, PeopleSoft® or any of the major enterprise applications.

Through the use of type-ahead, your company gets some great benefits:

* improving address data quality leading to significantly reduce returned mail;
* applying the same standards to address data will help reduce duplicates, since you won't be trying to compare "100 Main Street" to "One Hundred Main St.";
* users enter data faster. Addresses in the UK often just need a postal code, and the software will complete the rest of the address. Address entry in other countries will be faster too.

Vendors of this type of technology include QAS, Satori Software® and Melissa Data®. Data quality vendors like DataFlux™ and Trillium Software® also have real-time integration in many applications.

Workforce management

If you have a lot of people typing data into your systems, you may want to consider workforce management software. Most of the software in the space is an Orwellian attempt to police a call center. But there are applications that offer your call centers a helping hand – a parent showing you the way.

Your customer service representatives may be challenged by a mix of complicated and siloed applications, and constantly changing complex policies, procedures and product knowledge. The result is a call center that struggles with lack of adherence to processes, inaccurate information to customers and lack of standards when it comes to information quality. This type of technology will deliver relevant information to the call center employee, as it is smart enough to know where they are in the process and guide them step by step to the desired outcome for each call.

Vendors include Panviva.

Data quality dashboard

Data may not necessarily be coming into your databases via a call center or data entry. It may be coming into a centralized location from data feed or third-party vendors. Data quality dashboards allow you to keep an eye on data anomalies by constantly checking if the data meets business specifications. Dashboards offer attractive charts and graphs on the status of data compliance. They show your key performance indicators and trends conformity.

One client I worked with used data quality dashboards to monitor and report feeds from the company's many locations. The company was essentially a retail/service provider that wanted to ensure that client information was properly being entered into their database. Each night, the individual locations would report to the headquarters on the day's figures. The headquarters usually handled billing and therefore customer information was crucial.

With dashboards, the headquarters could report back to the individual data stewards and notify them when they got the data right and when they had allowed anomalies to get into the system. This feedback loop works to continually improve data quality, train data stewards at new locations and improve billing efficiency. Dashboards are also a great way to make your people smarter about data governance: they will help you achieve cleaner, more useful information.

In a previous chapter, I talked about aggregating the results of data anomalies from low-level dimensions like accuracy and completeness into higher-level business objectives like "Is my data ready to complete the mailing?" Dashboard applications are becoming more and more adroit at this. After all, they are essentially a presentation layer for data quality metrics, and they often can be adjusted to show business value.

Dashboard vendors include Dataflux, IBM, Informatica and Trillium Software.

Diagnostic and health

Commonly your organization will have years and years of data in storage. The damage has been done and it's the job of the data governance team to sort out the anomalies. Applications that are good at diagnosing and improving health are integral to a data governance program.

Data profiling

Not sure about the health and suitability of any given data set? Profile it, and you'll begin to understand how much data is missing, outlier values in the data and many other anomalies.

Data profiling is the start of understanding your data. It will tell you how many nulls there are in your customer_ID field, or what shape the data is in your PHONE field. It will help you identify the following types of issues:

- Data content issues – What are the minimum and maximum lengths of the table? What data type are the tables? What are the range of values? Are there any nulls? Is the table filled with the same value?
- Data structure issues – Is my primary key unique? Can I use anything else for a primary key? Does the metadata accurately describe the data?
- Data quality issues – Is the data accurate and complete? Does it follow our own data quality business rules?

It will not necessarily tell you if your customer database is ready for the June mailing. You have to work a bit to get that information.

Now you may be tempted to begin to write a bunch of queries to the database to do the job of the data profiling tool. Ad hoc methods of gathering metrics can be somewhat effective, but incomplete. The problem is that you really don't know what you don't know, so uncovering all the anomalies in a data set by using queries will be nearly impossible. The profiling tools tend to do a more systematic analysis of the data and help you avoid getting bit by a data inconsistency later in the project. Only when you understand all the anomalies will you be able to understand the scope of your data quality project.

Data profiling can be used by the team across the entire lifecycle of the project. You can use profiling to assess the data when you begin and reassess when you finish. This makes for some great chitchat in the data governance meetings. It's important to know how much you impacted data quality and the benefit of your team's work. You can use data profiling when you're moving data and merging it with other data sources. It's always great to know what the combined database will look like before you actually make the move.

Vendors include Dataflux, IBM, Informatica, Oracle, Pervasive®, Pitney Bowes Business Insight and Trillium Software.

Batch data quality

Once the anomalies are discovered, you can use batch data quality tools to fix them. A batch cleansing process can solve many problems with name and address data, supply chain data and more. Some solutions are batch-centric, while others can do both batch cleansing and scalable enterprise-class data quality (see below).

Data quality tools are the most underrated, yet amazing technologies in the data management world. I say that because these tools train a computer to do something it's not really designed to do – think. Computers are great for crunching numbers, loading and unloading data, etc. They are not so deft at thinking and making intelligent decisions. There's an artificial intelligence built in to data quality tools that make them fascinating.

Consider a database that contains the following records:

Record 1	Record 2
Peggy Johnson	Johnson, Margaret L.
345 6th Ave	345 Avenue of the
NY, NY 01012	Americas Manhattan, NY
	USA

If you carefully examine these two records, they are the same, or at least they refer to the same person. We know that Peggy is short for Margaret. We know that sometimes names come into the database comma reversed. We know that 6th Avenue was officially renamed Avenue of the Americas by the post office. We know that Manhattan is a borough of New York and that sometimes New York is abbreviated NY. All of these things rely on our knowledge, and that knowledge is not built in to any computer system or database that I'm familiar with.

Data quality tools have found a way to store up common anomalies in business rules libraries and identify them in a record. Through a series of steps, both records would be standardized as:

```
Margaret Johnson
345 Avenue of the
America
New York, NY 01012-1234
USA
```

This format is the standard format that the US postal service prefers. If we were to use normal computer comparison routines on the non-standardized records, there would be absolutely no way the records would match. However, the records do match up nicely after they are both standardized. We have found a duplicate record, which is a major contributor to data quality problems in customer databases.

By the way, we would never eliminate the original form of the record. Your customer may prefer to be addressed as "Peggy" in all her correspondence from you. The best strategy is to keep the original record and store the standardized form for matching and duplicate elimination.

While I'm on the topic of duplicate elimination, I should mention that matching technology is also an important part of data quality software. Matching's goal is to find the near-duplicates in the database. Is "Steven Smith" the same person as "Stephen Smyth" in your database? We'd use a series of algorithms plus other data associated with the record, like address, sex, tax ID number and so on, to make a determination.

I could go on about the wonderful things that data quality tools offer to improve information quality, but my point has been made. These tools offer powerful ways to improve and standardize both name and address and supply chain data.

Vendors include Dataflux, IBM, Informatica, Oracle, Group1, Silver Creek Systems® and Trillium Software.

Infrastructure

When we begin to talk about infrastructure, we need to look at metadata and ways to manage it. Metadata describes the infrastructure of your data. I said earlier in the book that I don't want to get too heavily into metadata, but it's at this point in the book that a definition of metadata is in order. Even members of the data governance team who are business line or executive should know the basic definition of metadata.

Metadata

The "soup can" metaphor is the best description of metadata that I've ever heard because it's easy to visualize. You go to the shelf and pick out a can of soup. On the label of a can is a nice picture of delicious-looking soup. The label gives nutritional information about the soup including the serving size and the size of the can. It may even also show other soups made by the company. So, if soup is the data, the metadata is the label on the can. In this case, since we have a lot of detail, we know exactly what to expect inside the can. You really want your metadata to be like that, giving any database engineer across your entire organization a good idea what's inside the can.

When metadata schema is set up, people don't always consider the going concern of the organization. In fact, they may get lazy and cause problems that will impact the corporation for years to come.

To continue with the soup can metaphor, what happens if you open the can and there's beef stew inside? It's a problem. Beef stew is like soup, but not exactly. Similarly, I can look at a database with a table labeled "FNAME" and expect that to be a person's first name. However, I shouldn't be surprised if FNAME contains a company name, two people's names (e.g. Jack and Diane) or a complete first and last name. In this case the metadata implies the contents, but may not always live up to the rule and that's a data quality problem.

On the other hand, what happens if the can is labeled ambiguously with something like "fry". It could mean that in order to prepare it, you have to fry it. It could mean that there are small fish in the can. It could be a can full of fried onion rings. You never know. I'm going to have to open the can to find out. Similarly, if we see ambiguous metadata, we are going to have to use data profiling technology to take a peek inside the can.

One final metadata example: let's say you have two cans labeled "soup." Can you assume that both cans contain the same kind of soup and that you can combine the cans to make a big batch? No, probably not. Similarly, you can't assume that tables with the same metadata label contain the same information. You can't assume that the databases will easily merge without some examination of both the metadata and the data itself. Data profiling technologies let us look inside the can and determine our process for merging.

ETL

ETL stands for "extract, transform and load" and it's used to migrate data from one database to another, to form data marts and data warehouses and also to convert databases from one format or type to another. Without getting too technical, ETL tools help you understand the metadata and transform data to a corporate standard.

ETL is generally thought of as a tool for extracting data from silos into a centralized data warehouse for the purpose of business intelligence.

Vendors include IBM, Informatica, Microsoft, Oracle, Business Objects®, SAS and SyncSort®.

Master data management

If there is one technology that underpins data governance, sets up a technical architect, than it's MDM software. Products from the mega-vendors like SAP and Oracle or products from smaller specialists like Siperian® and Tibco® provide MDM technology. MDM technologies feature, for example, data connectivity between applications, the ability to create a "gold" customer or supply chain record that can be shared between applications in a publish/subscribe model.

A big advantage for MDM technologies lies within their ability to connect to applications. The MDM solution can publish notification of change between applications. So, let's say that your call center CRM system receives a call from a customer who wants to place an order. The order and any changes to the contact information can be published to subscribing application like your ERP system and your billing system, thus maintaining a gold customer master throughout your systems.

MDM technologies provide the following features:

- **Workflow** – helps the data governance team manage data entry, exceptions processing issue escalation.
- **Metadata repository** – the database functions that set the data model in place and maintain it.
- **Security** – handles who can access to the data.
- **History** – lets the solution track changes to the database over time. Keeping track of historical data is often a requirement for compliance.
- **Connectivity** – allows data to flow and sync up between subscribing applications with a publish/subscribe model.

- **Data quality** – allows connectivity to an enterprise-level data quality solution. Some MDM solutions have their own simple data quality features built in, like rudimentary matching, or you can buy a more industrial-strength data quality tool from a data quality vendor.

Strictly speaking of technologies and not MDM methodologies, MDM is a data integration application that solves business problems. These applications add value providing business-specific metadata models that can be used by the corporation. The models might be vertically focused, like a metadata model for pharmaceutical companies, or it may be focused on data type, like customer data versus supply chain data.

Vendors include IBM, Initiate Systems®, Oracle, Siperian and Tibco.

Enterprise-class data quality

Enterprise-class data quality tools provide real-time data quality to any application in the enterprise, including the MDM solution. Beyond the desktop data quality system, the enterprise-class system should be fast enough and scalable enough to provide an instant check of information quality in almost any application with any number of users.

Enterprise-class data quality tools are all about supporting the data governance initiative by being able to replicate and scale. This class of data quality tools support replication and portability across practically any platform or system. They let you leverage efforts from one data governance project across new projects and the entire enterprise, dramatically reducing costs in multiple implementations and allowing you to easily create an enterprise data quality standard.

Vendors include IBM, Trillium Software and Dataflux.

Data monitoring

You can often use the same technology to monitor data as you do for profiling data. These tools keep track of the quality of the data. Unlike data quality dashboards, the IT staff can really dig into the detail if necessary.

Enrichment

Services and data sources

Companies like Harte-Hanks offer data sources that can help fill the gaps when mission-critical data is missing. You can buy data and services to segment your database, check customer lists for change of address, look for customers on the do-not-call list, reverse phone number look-ups and more.

Vendors include Harte-Hanks, Dun & Bradstreet, Acxiom®, Data Mentors™ and Experian®.

CHAPTER 9: THE AUDACITY OF DATA GOVERNANCE

We understand that like many things in life, data governance does not come easy. Data governance is earned with slow and incremental change by those who have the forethought to see the future and by those who know that success relies upon accurate corporate information.

For companies, choosing whether to embark on data governance, it is a choice between chaos and order. Most companies want to own their market, meaning they want to be the top dog in their space – the Google, Toyota and Apple iPod of their worlds. But how can you own your market if all you own is disorder? By making order out of chaotic information, data governance is the coin counting machine that turns your scattered data coins into real assets.

In fact, those companies succeeding in this data-centric world are treating their data assets just as they would treat cold, hard cash. With data governance, companies strive to protect their ecosystem of data like it is a monetary system. It can't be the data center's problem alone: it has to be everyone's responsibility throughout the entire company.

But data governance has to be about more than just money. The choice about data governance is one about hearing the voices of your people. The sound of bad harmonization and discord can be heard loudly in companies that don't listen to it. It's only when you harmonize the voices of technologists, executives and business teams that it allows you to produce a beautiful song; one that can bring your company teamwork, strategic direction and profit.

9: The Audacity of Data Governance

On an emotional level, the move toward data governance is really a choice between optimism and fear. Does the modern-day lifeblood of your corporation – data – drive hope in all that it can provide your company, or does it shape fear with your corporate imagination? When your workers think about your data, are they haunted by a never-ending vision that there will only will be more data, more mergers and more complexity in the years to come, or are they hopeful that the future will bring more opportunity, more efficiency and a more agile working environment? Are they worried about the accuracy of reports and making faulty decisions, or are they confident that they have all the metrics they need to make good decisions? When you choose data governance, you choose *hope*.

CHAPTER 10: CASE STUDY – BT

Perhaps one the most successful case studies in data governance and data quality improvement is that of British Telecommunications Group plc, also known as BT. One of the largest communication companies in the world, BT serves well over 20 million customers worldwide, most of them in Europe. From a data management perspective, BT is typical of a big and complex company, having grown over the decades through merger of government-controlled agencies, privatization, natural growth and acquisition. By 1997, BT's growth and history had spawned over 700 operational systems organized around product lines.

It was then that the team at BT looked around and began to realize that the silos of data did not meet their business objectives. They realized that having a 360 degree customer view, the ability to see customers across product lines, was going to be crucial to being an effective, customer-centric organization. They realized that to accomplish this vision, they would have to consolidate data. Success in migrating the data from the separate systems into a consolidated view was heavily dependant on proper data management. BT knew that the migration projects could fail if they didn't account for differences in data across operational systems.

But data issues went beyond a consolidated view of customers. BT also wanted to look at assets, things like private circuits (lines) that existed in the real world, but were undocumented and therefore did not exist in their systems. After all, an asset is only an asset if you know it exists. This failure to document inventory assets drove up capital expenditure, as they were forced to create new, but unnecessary circuits, rather than reuse capacity freed up elsewhere.

BT had internal perception problems, too. Business leaders in the corporation did not see investments in IT as successful as they should have been. Even after new IT systems were implemented, it took too long to launch related products and services. Finally, the company was trying to comply with the EU Data Protection Act, an edict that lays down strict rules around data storage and usage. Key was that data held must be accurate. If not, the customer has a right to insist on corrections across all systems where that data was held. If records appeared across many systems, this would be very difficult to do.

Meager beginnings

BT started small in setting up their first information quality program. It was initiated with two people, one in business and one in IT. One of the first things that the small team set out to do was to interview 30 key stakeholders, both business people and executives, to identify where data quality was hurting the company. They decided to begin to form a common methodology and a common toolset to make sure data quality projects would be reusable and expandable. They kicked off some pilots, then moved them into operational-scale projects. In the beginning, BT picked high-value, high-ROI projects while keeping the entire organization's data needs in mind.

The BT team started their data governance program in marketing, cleansing the large customer base in batch cleansing processes. They then moved on to real-time validation of name and address information as it came in from the call centers and other sources. These projects began to move the company toward a company-wide single view of customers. The team then advanced to other data issues, like the inventory management system. In the data quality process, they recovered lost assets, like private circuits, and were able to put them back into service.

In picking projects, BT developed a robust process. They first used data profiling tools to diagnose issues. From there, they built a business case for improvement. Only if the business case was approved was a solution designed and deployed. BT says there were times where a potential project could not have achieved a positive ROI and therefore they held off until higher value projects were first completed. There were also times where there was a phased approach, fixing certain aspects of the data in phase one and going back again later to fix more.

BT made some important decisions early on. Even early in the data governance program, they developed a clear definition of what was meant by good quality information: BT used the term "Peak Condition Information" to describe data that was not only accurate, complete and reliable, but was fit for purpose, accessible and timely. They realized early on that all the terabytes of data could not be always made 100% accurate, but as long as it was fit-for-purpose, it would be more valuable to the organization.

Organizationally, the company drove the program by setting up an enterprise-wide Information Management Forum, comprising a business champion in each line of business as well as one in the CIO team. They set in place a comprehensive communication plan. They encouraged people to stop doing their own data cleansing because cleansing alone was reactive, not proactive. The results of renegade cleansing could actually make things worse, as each team's cleansing resulted in a potentially different definition of good quality.

From a tools perspective, they leveraged data quality tools and data profiling tools to accomplish effective data management. They trained consultants to learn the tools and the business processes. They expanded further by creating an IT center of excellence which leveraged these common methods and tools. Eventually, they moved all the IT people working on data quality into this center of excellence, rather than having them in business unit silos.

The benefits were huge. The company improved the efficiencies of asset management, operational and customer service systems. In the front office, morale improved, staff turnover was reduced, and they were more confident in dealing with regulations like the EU Data Protection Act.

Over ten years, the data governance team demonstrated just how very valuable they were to the organization and the team grew to over 50 people who completed over 75 data quality improvement projects. Today, BT is a much-lauded data governance case study and even a data quality practice that is sold as a consulting service to companies across Europe and the world.

As for return on investment, the numbers are staggering. BT saved about $106 million in their meager efforts up to 2002. They really got going in 2003 and 2004, when they were able to save nearly another $400 million. Data management projects are still going on today, although the data quality components are baked into the projects as part of new application roll-outs. Over the years since 2000, BT has documented over a billion dollars in savings due to better data management.

Lessons learned

The lessons we learn from BT are that there's only one measure that matters when it comes to proving the value of data governance – money. You can start your data governance initiative today by just doing something, no matter how small, to show the ROI of data management. Once you do, work with the business stakeholders to help you sell the importance of data governance. If you can make it clear that data quality is everyone's problem, the whole company wins.

ITG RESOURCES

IT Governance Ltd sources, creates and delivers products and services to meet the real-world, evolving IT governance needs of today's organizations, directors, managers and practitioners. The ITG website (*www.itgovernance.co.uk*) is the international one-stop-shop for corporate and IT governance information, advice, guidance, books, tools, training and consultancy.

www.itgovernanceusa.com provides a complete range of IT governance books and tools into North America from our US logistics base.

www.27001.com is our information security-focused website that deals specifically with information security issues in a North American context.

Pocket Guides

For full details of the entire range of pocket guides, simply follow the links at *www.itgovernance.co.uk/publishing.aspx.*

Toolkits

ITG's unique range of toolkits includes the IT Governance Framework Toolkit, which contains all the tools and guidance that you will need in order to develop and implement an appropriate IT governance framework for your organization. Full details can be found at *www.itgovernance.co.uk/products/519*.

For a free paper on how to use the proprietary Calder-Moir IT Governance Framework, and for a free trial version of the toolkit, see *www.itgovernance.co.uk/calder_moir.aspx.*

Best Practice Reports

ITG's new range of Best Practice Reports is now at: *www.itgovernance.co.uk/best-practice-reports.aspx*. These offer you essential, pertinent, expertly researched information on an increasing number of key issues.

Training and Consultancy

IT Governance also offers training and consultancy services across the entire spectrum of disciplines in the information governance arena. Details of training courses can be accessed at *www.itgovernance.co.uk/training.aspx* and descriptions of our consultancy services can be found at *www.itgovernance.co.uk/consulting.aspx*.

Why not contact us to see how we could help you and your organization?

Newsletter

IT governance is one of the hottest topics in business today, not least because it is also the fastest moving, so what better way to keep up than by subscribing to ITG's free monthly newsletter, *Sentinel*? It provides monthly updates and resources across the whole spectrum of IT governance subject matter, including risk management, information security, ITIL and IT service management, project governance, compliance and so much more. Subscribe for your free copy at: *www.itgovernance.co.uk/newsletter.aspx*.

CPSIA information can be obtained at www.ICGtesting.com
Printed in the USA
BVOW071105241011

274391BV00002B/31/P